PRAISE FOR *VISIONARY BUSINESS*

"This breakthrough book can show you not only how to envision and create success, but also how to build a truly visionary business, one that supports its employees and even the community and the environment....*Visionary Business* will prove to be a significant book for the twenty-first century."
— *The Real Entrepreneur*

"Offers valuable insights to any new entrepreneur....Allen's central message is this: being a visionary goes beyond minding the bottom line; it is possible to pursue one's true dreams and cultivate a successful business."
— *Whole Life Times*

"Inspiration and insights for entrepreneurs everywhere. Every so often a book comes along that really changes the way you think about business."
— *Working Solo*

"Marc Allen's business experience and humor shine through his guide to entrepreneurial success, lighting a way for all who seek the joy and challenge of independence."
— Nancy Anderson, author of *Work with Passion*

"An inspiring book about business by someone who truly walks the talk."
— Carol Orsborn, author of *The Art of Resilience*

PRAISE FOR MARC ALLEN'S
THE MILLIONAIRE COURSE

"The world needs you to fulfill your financial potential and become a compassionate giver and make-it-happen millionaire. My friend Marc Allen teaches you how to become an 'enlightened millionaire.' I love his brilliant insights."
— Mark Victor Hansen,
co-creator of the *Chicken Soup for the Soul* series

"Marc Allen is now reaching a wide range of people who are serious about positively changing their lives and the world.... The book is filled with practical wisdom that can help you create a fulfilled life."
— Shakti Gawain, author of *Creative Visualization*

PRAISE FOR MARC ALLEN'S
THE GREATEST SECRET OF ALL

"*The Greatest Secret of All* is a wonderful contribution to humanity. It sounds a new note that has universal resonance, and gives us the key to a life well lived."
— Gay Hendricks, author of *Conscious Loving* and *Five Wishes*

"Few teachers get my attention like Marc Allen.... He takes lofty success principles and brings them to earth in simple yet compelling ways. I have tried the principles he suggests in this book, and they really work. They will work for you, too. Success books don't get any easier than this — or more effective."
— Alan Cohen, author of *Relax into Wealth*

"There are no secrets, but there are things we cannot or will not see and accept because of our life experience. This book can help you to see what is no secret but what has remained hidden from your awareness, and the result will be to profoundly change your life."
— Dr. Bernie S. Siegel, author of
Love, Medicine and Miracles and *365 Prescriptions for the Soul*

VISIONARY
BUSINESS

ALSO BY MARC ALLEN

VISIONARY BUSINESS

An Entrepreneur's Guide to Success

REVISED EDITION

MARC ALLEN

NEW WORLD LIBRARY
NOVATO, CALIFORNIA

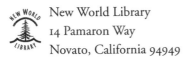

New World Library
14 Pamaron Way
Novato, California 94949

Edited by Gina Misiroglu, Paula Dragosh, and Kristen Cashman
Text design by Tona Pearce Myers
Cover design by Mary Ann Casler

Library of Congress Cataloging-in-Publication Data
Allen, Marc.
Visionary business : an entrepreneur's guide to success / Marc Allen. — Rev. ed.
    p.   cm.
ISBN 978-1-57731-662-6 (pbk. : alk. paper)
1. Success in business. 2. Entrepreneurship. 3. Management. I. Title.
HF5386.A535 2008
658.4'09—dc22   2008053607

First printing, April 2009
ISBN 978-1-57731-662-6
Printed in the United States on 30% postconsumer-waste recycled paper

New World Library is a proud member of the Green Press Initiative.

10   9   8   7   6   5   4   3   2   1

Dedicated to all those who dare to dream,

and all those who have the knowledge, generosity,

and heart to support others in reaching their dreams.

Keep away from people who try to belittle your ambitions.

Small people always do that, but the really great

make you feel that you, too,

can somehow become great.

— MARK TWAIN

CONTENTS

VISIONARY
BUSINESS

INTRODUCTION

THIS IS A FICTIONALIZED ACCOUNT of a true story. There really was a Bernie, the central prophet in this tale of wisdom, though somewhere in the telling of the story his character grew and merged with several other people I have met along the way, including a wonderful man named Michael Bliss, who was ninety years young when I met him, still teaching piano and cello, and inspiring all who came around to his little house in Malibu, California.

I have not adhered very closely to the actual facts of my story but have focused more on the principles and the keys of visionary business — the keys that have been given to me, one by one, over the years from a variety of sources.

The first edition of *Visionary Business* proved beyond a doubt that this book can help a great many people not only to improve their businesses and the quality of their lives, but also to make this world a better place for all. For that is the ultimate goal of a visionary business: to transform the world, by doing what we love to do, into an ecologically sustainable environment, with peace and plenty for all.

KEY ONE

Imagine your ideal scene.

Many years ago, with the help of a few friends, I started my own business. We were like most founders of small businesses: full of dreams, but short of concrete business experience; full of ideas, but short of cash. We were overworked and underpaid. We were overwhelmed much of the time, and seriously undercapitalized.

We had a great many vague ideals, but had never written a mission statement. We had high hopes, but had never written a business plan.

We set up a small office and furnished it with the bare necessities to take care of business. All three of us continued to work at other jobs, part-time, and poured as much cash as we could into our little start-up. All of our savings (which wasn't much) went into the company. A few friends and relatives invested along the way, and a few others loaned us money. But the money always went quickly, and we were continually strapped for cash.

For those who loaned us money, we made a clear payment schedule, and we made those payments a priority. But that brought with it more pressures to pay more out every month.

For those who invested, we promised a share of ownership in the company. They would become stockholders and officially own some portion of something, as soon as we got around to incorporating. But month after month passed, and we never got around to setting up a corporation. We were too swept up in the vast number of never-ending daily details that had to be handled to be able to step back and do any long-term planning.

One of our first employees quit; he said there was too much stress in the company and too little security. He didn't want to worry about whether his paycheck would be good every pay period. I couldn't blame him; he wasn't getting paid enough to deal with the level of anxiety in that little office. None of us were, but at least those of us who were owners had the possibility of having something of value in a distant, vaguely fantasized future.

My other job was flexible freelance work I was able to do right in my office, so I was there nearly every day, but I always had the feeling that I needed to give my little start-up more hours than I could give it. Everything was constantly behind schedule; we kept missing important deadlines we needed to make in order to get our projects done on time.

I always tried to get out of the office in the morning and again in the afternoon for at least a brief walk. I usually found some kind of errand that needed to be run, or sometimes I would just walk around the block. I needed to get out of that confined, cluttered space to do some thinking, to clear my head of the endless details that threatened to overwhelm me at times.

ONE MORNING, AS I LEFT THE OFFICE, I saw an old man sitting on a bench across the street. He caught my eye because he was motionless, gazing into space ... an old man, far away. When I came back from my walk, he was sitting in exactly the same position. Apparently he hadn't moved a muscle. He was looking in the general direction of our office, but his gaze seemed way beyond any specific focus.

His eyes and facial expression reminded me of something, but I couldn't remember what. It was quiet, reflective. Maybe there was a touch of sadness — but maybe that was just my projection. There was definitely a touch of humor. He looked familiar, but I couldn't remember why.

I saw him a few times after that, always sitting in the same position. I don't think I ever saw him move. I wondered if he was waiting for something — a ride? Godot? Nothing?

He looked so familiar ... then I remembered where I had seen those eyes, and that expression: on the Yoda doll on my dresser — the Jedi master from the *Star Wars* movies. The old man was striking in his silence and stillness.

THEN ONE DAY he came strolling through the door of our little office. I seem to recall it was a beautiful spring day, though I hadn't paid much attention to it. My attention had been on the crisis of the day. I don't even remember now the particular crisis — each day had its own problems. About all we were doing was crisis management: dealing with one demanding situation after another.

He breezed in the door, uninvited and certainly unexpected. He was wearing a brown old-man suit, with brown shoes — quite conservative dress. Nobody knew who he was. He stood there, hands in his pockets, and carefully looked around the office. He looked as if he almost expected us to welcome him, as if he had an appointment with someone.

He had sharp features, and his wavy white hair was combed straight back, with a substantial amount of gel. His skin seemed taut on his face; he was old, but it was impossible to tell his age. At first it looked like he didn't have a wrinkle on his face, but as he turned into the light, I could see his delicate skin was covered with fine lines.

I walked over to him.

"Can I help you?" I said.

"I don't know," he said with a smile. He held out his hand. "My name's Bernie."

I shook his hand; his fingers were long and delicate and cool. There was something warm and friendly about the old guy, something that immediately put me at ease.

"I'm Marc."

"Nice little business you've got here."

"Well, it's just a beginning, I hope."

"How long have you been in business?"

"Oh, we've had the office about six months, though we've been working on it for over a year now — no, wait, it's been almost two years now." I flushed, a bit embarrassed — where had the time gone?

"I like the way you've furnished the office."

He said it with a smile; I didn't know if he was kidding or not. The office furniture was a hodgepodge of the cheapest stuff we could find at flea markets and garage sales, with a few leftovers from our apartments thrown in. Our front desk was a sheet of plywood with two-by-fours for legs.

"It's low cost," I said.

"That's what I like about it," he said. "I've seen start-ups that have put all their money into the furniture. I invested in a company a while ago, and the two owners went out and bought Mercedes and custom-built oak desks. I couldn't believe it! They even had *custom-built bookcases!* I told 'em they needed to spend their money on their business, not on their furniture. They promised me they'd be fine — and they went bankrupt before the year was out. They didn't invest in the future."

He looked around the office, then spoke with a sudden vehemence.

"As a start-up, you've got to spend wisely. Every bit of capital you've got is precious, and you've got to use it on the

things that'll make your company grow. And don't buy a
Mercedes until you can easily afford it."

His story piqued my interest. I didn't know what to say;
there was a pause that felt awkward to me. He simply
looked at me, carefully, with that slight smile of his. I felt as
if he were assessing something, but I had no idea what.

"Are you looking for an investor?" He said it casually,
giving it no more importance than if he was asking me for
the time of day.

"Well...we could use some capital..."

"Do you have a business plan?"

"Ah...no, not really. Lots of ideas, and plans of course,
but nothing really concrete on paper yet."

I suddenly became aware that we were both standing,
somewhat awkwardly, near the doorway. At least I felt awkward. Bernie seemed supremely comfortable, with his hands
in his pockets.

"Would you like some coffee or something?" I said.
"Would you like to sit down?"

"Sounds good to me."

I gave Bernie a quick tour of the office — it certainly
didn't take long to see the entire operation — and we got
some coffee and sat down in my little room in the back.
Bernie liked his coffee loaded with milk and sugar. As he
stirred it in, I noticed the cuff links he sported: large, one-
ounce gold coins. And his tie tack was made out of one of
the biggest gold nuggets I had ever seen.

He didn't waste time getting down to business. "You
need a plan," he said. "I might invest; I might not. You don't

know me from Adam — I could be a weirdo off the street who's conning you for a free cup of coffee." He said it with his enigmatic smile. He could have been speaking the truth — I had no idea.

"But it doesn't matter. If all I do is encourage you to get started on a plan, my little visit here will have been worth your time. You need a solid, well-written business plan before any investor will take you seriously. Every company needs a plan, whether they need investors or not. A business without a plan is like a ship without a course. You just wander around aimlessly, without reaching any destination, because you haven't charted out the course necessary to get anywhere. You haven't even determined your destination.

"Your plan doesn't have to be long and involved; it doesn't have to be complex. But it has to be clear, to you and to anyone else who's interested.

"Start with a brief, concise summary, on less than a page. Tell us what your company does, how much cash you need, your projected growth, and how you're going to structure the return on investment — is it a loan repaid with interest? Or is it equity in the company, getting a certain share of the profits?"

"It could be either," I said.

"That's fine. It's good to have some options. Give us your summary on one page and on the next page give us your mission statement. Make it as idealistic as you can, as grand as you want. Then describe your business in more detail in the next few pages: what it is, what you do as a company.

Put it in simple words, so it's understandable to someone who's not familiar with your industry. Show us where you're at, as of today. Tell us who is involved and what you do. Then tell us where you want to be in a year, two years, and five years — and show us your map for getting there.

"First do it as simply as possible — and briefly as possible — in words; then show us with numbers. Show us your cash-flow projections for the next five years. It should be clear how much capital you're going to need, what you're going to do with it, and what results you predict."

"Okay," I said. I grabbed some paper and started making some notes. This guy may have been a wacko, but he was giving some very good advice.

"But, you know, I want to suggest doing one thing first, even before you do your plan — a great exercise that'll help you with your plan, among other things. How many people work here?"

"A total of five. Plus a part-time bookkeeper."

"How many of you are owners?"

"The three of us who started the company."

"The other two are paid employees?"

"Right. The owners don't draw anything out of the company yet."

"How are you set up? A partnership?"

I hesitated. "Yeah, though we haven't really finalized the agreement."

Bernie looked at me oddly, coldly. His eyes were a pale gray, almost luminescent. "Partnerships don't work," he said flatly.

"What do you mean?" I said. "There have been lots of successful partnerships."

"Name two."

I laughed. I knew there were many, many successful partnerships in the world — but I couldn't think of any at the moment. Bernie seemed to enjoy watching me squirm.

"What about law firms, and accounting firms?" I said. "Aren't they partnerships?"

"Oh, there are a lot of successful businesses organized as partnerships," Bernie said, completely contradicting himself. "But they don't operate as partnerships."

He left it there, as if it should be obvious to me. It wasn't.

"What do you mean?" I said.

"A partnership usually means two or more people are responsible, ultimately, for the company, right? For the executive decisions. And over time, two or more people will never agree on everything. There are always disagreements; there will always be conflict. Even if the business is organized as a partnership, legally, one person has to be the president. One person has to make the final decisions. One person has to be responsible for the success or failure of the business."

I didn't know if I agreed with his sweeping generalizations.

"Why?" I asked.

"Because partnerships don't work." He smiled; he seemed on the verge of laughter. His smugness was a little irritating. So was his logic.

"Look — how often has it happened in your company that one of the partners assumes the other is responsible for something, only to find that the other one has assumed someone else is responsible — and something important hasn't been taken care of? Has that ever happened to you?"

I had to admit it had, all too many times.

"That's the nature of partnerships," he said. "No one is fully responsible for the whole picture. So things get neglected. The ball gets dropped, because no one person is responsible for that ball being carried the whole distance. And another thing that always happens — *always* happens — is that one partner will feel they're putting in more time, and energy, and maybe even money, than the other. There's never an equal balance — that's impossible to achieve. One person always feels they're carrying a greater load than the other."

I had to admit I'd had those feelings as well.

"I suggest you form a corporation — an LLC is easy to set up — and put one person in charge."

I jotted down "LLC" in my notebook; I didn't want to interrupt Bernie, and didn't want him to know I had no idea what an LLC was. (Later on, I looked it up: It means "Limited Liability Corporation," and it's far easier to set up than a traditional corporation.)

"Or if it seems premature to form a corporation, at least choose someone to be president. Some people resist this, saying it's hierarchical, but in my experience I've found it's practical. It's efficient. It works. And it doesn't necessarily have to be hierarchical. The president doesn't have to be the boss, and tell everyone else what to do. But one person has to carry the vision of success, and has to be responsible for realizing that vision. The others can be on the board of directors; they can head different departments, different divisions that reflect their area of expertise — but the buck has got to stop somewhere, with one person. If you want to be egalitarian, or whatever you want to call it, or if you have two strong leaders, you could even rotate the leadership role. But at every moment, one person has to be in charge."

"I can see your point."

"Good. Now here's the little exercise I'd suggest you do, before you do your business plan — and it may help you determine who's going to be president, if it isn't already obvious. It'll certainly help you with your business plan.

"Have everyone in the company sit down — or at least have the owners sit down, if the other employees are uncomfortable with this — and have everybody write down, on paper, *exactly what they want to be doing five years from now.*

"Assume that your business has grown according to plan — in fact assume that everything has gone really well, and you've been successful — then ask yourself what you'd like to be doing. What's your *ideal scene?* What if money were no object, what if you could have exactly the kind of life you wanted, what would it be?

"Put it in writing, and read it to each other. Do this before you write your business plan. You'll be in for some revelations."

He finished his coffee. We exchanged cards, and he

strolled out the front door. I still had no idea what to think of him. He could have been an old man living in a fantasy world, for all I knew. But he had a business card, and it read:

UIC
UNIVERSAL INVESTMENT CORPORATION

That sounded promising. An address and phone number followed; the address looked like it was a room or suite in a hotel.

We did the little exercise Bernie suggested, and dubbed it the "ideal scene process." All five of us in our little company sat down and described, on paper, the kind of life we wanted to be living five years in the future, assuming everything had gone as well as we could imagine.

Bernie was right: We were in for some revelations. I was the only one of the three owners who even wanted to be running the business five years in the future. The other two wanted to use the business as a springboard to launch them into other creative careers. The exercise helped us put not only the future but also the present into a clearer perspective. I became the president of the company, focusing on new product development; the other two became vice presidents in charge of marketing and operations, respectively.

It became my responsibility to write the business plan — with a lot of help from my friends, of course. I needed a lot of help, especially on the financial side.

SUMMARY

- A start-up company should spend money only on the things that will make the company grow.

- Every company needs a business plan, whether or not it needs investors. A business without a plan is like a ship without a course.

- Your business plan doesn't have to be long and involved, but it has to be in writing and clear, to you and to anyone else who reads it. Start your plan with a one-page summary, then have a brief, concise mission statement. Make it as idealistic as you can, as grand as you want. A mission statement helps the company retain its focus and can be crucial in determining the company's direction and even its level of success.

- After the summary and mission statement, describe your business and your present circumstances; then describe where you want to be in a year, two years, and five years — and present a map for getting there. First do it as simply as possible in words, then in numbers. End with cash-flow projections that show you exactly how much capital you need to raise.

- Remember that partnerships work only in unique situations; most businesses that operate as partnerships run into difficulties. One person has to be

completely responsible for the success or failure of
the business.

• Be sure the owners — and, ideally, all the employees as well — write their "ideal scenes" down on
paper, and compare notes: What do you want to be
doing five years from now, assuming that your business has grown according to plan? What would your
life look like? What would you be doing? Where
would you live? What would a typical day look like?
This simple exercise is a powerful visionary tool.

KEY TWO

*Write your business plan
as a simple, clear visualization.*

W RITING THE BUSINESS PLAN was not an easy task. The financial projections were especially difficult; I needed a great deal of assistance from a great many people to make realistic projections. It took far more time than I thought it would.

Bernie had told me to make monthly projections for the first year or two, then quarterly projections for the rest. We had to imagine every conceivable expense, as accurately as possible. Finances were never my strong point; making all those projections was no fun at all. I continually had the feeling that I was forgetting something important, something that would change everything. And I kept discovering new expenses, and they seemed exorbitant and overwhelming. Taxes — federal, state, county, and sales taxes. All the additional things added to payroll — the list seemed endless. Insurance — we needed far more than we had. Accounting. Legal advice.

The projections for income were nerve-racking as well: Who had any idea what our income would be five years in the future? Or one year? Or six months? I was pulling projections out of the clear blue sky, and fearing I was being far too optimistic. Yet if I was less optimistic, I couldn't see a way to become profitable. It was a dilemma that kept me awake at night.

It took several long months to complete the projections. I hadn't heard a word from Bernie. I called him and got an answering machine. I left a message, and Bernie got back to me the next day. He told me to bring the business plan and meet him at his office. It felt like a special day — I even put on a sport coat for the occasion.

BERNIE'S "OFFICE" TURNED OUT TO BE A SUITE in a hotel on the mezzanine floor with a large balcony in front of his door that looked out over the lobby. He said he liked to have his office in a hotel because they had room service. We sat on big stuffed chairs on the balcony and gazed at the scene below, all the people coming and going, and had lunch delivered to us. Bernie had a ham sandwich on white bread and coffee with a heavy dose of sugar and milk.

I felt quite a bit of trepidation as I handed him the business plan. According to our cash-flow projections, we were going to need quite an infusion of capital — and soon — if we were going to reach our goals. Or even if we were going to stay in business, because we were losing money every month. Without some outside financing, the future looked pretty bleak.

Bernie read through it quickly, skimming most parts. He gave the financial pages a bit more of a thorough reading, though he seemed to just glance over most of the specifics and focus more intently on a few select numbers. I sat fidgeting as he read in silence.

"It's a good start," he said finally, still staring at the numbers. "You've done your homework."

I smiled, and swelled a bit with satisfaction.

"But I want you to rewrite it."

My swelling quickly fizzled. "What's wrong with it?" I asked.

"Nothing's terribly wrong — but you don't have enough contingencies built in. Things rarely happen as we project them to happen. There are always contingencies, unexpected developments, unforeseen problems — and they usually cost money.

"I have a rule of thumb: Everything in a start-up business will take twice as long and cost twice as much as you expect. This may sound pessimistic, but it's based on experience. The single biggest problem small start-up companies face is that they project they need x number of dollars, and they raise x number of dollars, and then they spend it and still need more cash. But their investors have already put in all they intend to, and the company has blown its credibility by not performing as it said it would. I've seen so many companies collapse that were 90 percent there, so close to making it, but they just couldn't raise that last 10 percent of capital they needed. The well was dry. They had lost the trust of their investors.

"Make sure your plan is realistic. Make sure you're asking for plenty of capital, enough to cover every imaginable contingency. And at the bottom of your expense pages, add another 15 percent or so for contingencies — unforeseen expenses. Okay?"

"Okay." I was not too happy at the thought of rewriting the plan, and I couldn't help but feel that, if we did as Bernie suggested, we might be in need of so much money that we would never find anyone with the resources to invest that much.

And there was another fear, one that had kept me awake more than a few nights: If we really did need twice as much as we were projecting, how could we make enough of a profit so the investors would get some kind of reasonable return on investment? Bernie seemed to read my mind.

"Don't worry about asking for what might seem like a lot of money. And don't worry, at this point, about return on investment. Let your investors deal with that. You need to create a document you can work with.

"A well-written business plan is far more than a tool for raising money. This plan is your map, your visualization of the future." He held it up as he said it, and his big ounce-of-gold cuff links flashed in the light. I couldn't help smiling as he said "visualization" — it seemed so uncharacteristic for an old man in a brown suit, even though his cuff links and big gold-nugget tie tack were far from conservative.

"The clearer, the more concrete, the visualization, the greater the chance of achieving it. You need a plan that not only makes sense financially, but feels achievable, on a gut level. You need a plan that is clear and strong enough to seep deeply into your subconscious mind. That sets the whole universe in motion to bring about the results you desire.

"Your plan has to be strong enough to overcome every hurdle and obstacle, external and internal — external problems like lack of capital, competition, changes in the marketplace and economy, as well as your own internal obstacles of fear, doubt, lack of confidence or self-esteem, lack of experience and knowledge, and so on.

"Here's something to remember: The internal obstacles are the most important ones to deal with. Get the inside right and the outside will take care of itself."

Bernie seemed positively radiant. He looked about twenty years younger, filled with vitality, as he spoke.

"This plan is powerful! Because it's capable of setting your powerful subconscious mind in motion!

"Once you have a clear plan, nothing can stop you — except yourself, or unless you're violating some basic universal laws, laws that are obvious to anyone with some ethics or common sense.

"I want to see you do one more thing, too: Summarize your plan in *one page*. It's good for your investors, but far more important for *you*. Keep it in mind. Read it often.

When you write the key points down on a single page, it's something your subconscious mind can easily grasp, and get to work on.

"Once you have a clear plan, written on one page and etched in your brain, you turn your desire for success into an *intention*. Once you have the intention to succeed, 90 percent of the things you imagine to be obstacles will dissolve, and you'll have the tools to deal with the other 10 percent as they come up. In fact, those obstacles can become opportunities once you have a clear intention — within every problem you can see an opportunity.

"Don't forget that: Turn your desires into intentions; turn your obstacles and problems into opportunities and benefits. I have a big sign over my desk that reads: *'For every adversity, there's the seed of an equal or greater benefit.'* Napoleon Hill said that.

"For every problem, there's an opportunity. *'Even in the knocks of life, we can find great gifts'* — that's from the Bhagavad Gita, written thousands of years ago. So there's nothing new in this.

"Another way to say it is a popular cliché — but it's one of our best clichés, because it's true: *Where there's a will, there's a way.*"

He gave me that same look he'd given me the day we met — as if he was assessing something within me.

"I don't think you've got anything to worry about," he said, somewhat ambiguously. "Let's call room service and have some dessert. Or at least some more coffee."

SUMMARY

- Write a clear and concrete business plan. Make monthly projections for the first year or two, then quarterly projections for the rest.

- Build contingencies into your plan. Try to imagine every possible expense, then total all expenses and add another 15 percent or so to that total for unforeseen expenses.

- Remember this rule of thumb: Things in a start-up business could take twice as long and cost twice as much as you expect. Be sure to plan to have enough resources to overcome delays and unexpected expenses.

- A well-written business plan is far more than a tool for raising money: It is your map, your visualization of the future. Summarize your plan in one page, and read it often. The clearer, the more concrete the visualization, the greater your chance of achieving it.

- Your plan has to be strong enough to overcome every hurdle and obstacle, external and internal. A business plan is powerful, because it sets in motion your powerful subconscious mind.

- A well-written business plan turns your desire for success into an *intention*. Once you have the intention to succeed, 90 percent of your perceived obstacles will dissolve, and you will have the tools to deal with the other 10 percent as they come up.

• Turn your desires into intentions; turn your obstacles and problems into opportunities and benefits. *"For every adversity, there is the seed of an equal or greater benefit"* — Napoleon Hill. Within every problem is an opportunity. *"Even in the knocks of life, we can find great gifts"* — the Bhagavad Gita. Another way to phrase this has been a part of our language for a long time: *Where there's a will, there's a way.*

KEY THREE

Discover your higher purpose.

Bᴇʀɴɪᴇ'ꜱ ʟɪᴛᴛʟᴇ ᴛᴀʟᴋ ꜱᴜʀᴘʀɪꜱᴇᴅ ᴍᴇ. Here was this old man, by almost anyone's standards — I had no idea how old he was, but he was well over seventy — talking about visualization, and your subconscious mind. But his words were inspiring — and his office suite proved he had attained some degree of success. I made some notes after our meeting, so I'd remember his advice.

I went back to the business plan and wrestled with it some more. I could see that Bernie was right in one respect: I began to see how the plan was our visualization of a possible future.

You could say the first exercise he had suggested to us, the "ideal scene process," was just a fantasy, but it certainly was a stretching of the imagination that forced us to look at the big picture, which is invaluable.

Working on the business plan, however, brought that fantasy down into concrete terms. As I completed the revision of it, I felt that I was much closer to achieving it, somehow, maybe even halfway toward it. I felt, too, that I had already completed the most difficult part, or at least the most essential part. For every flight needs a flight plan and a destination.

Not long after I started reworking the business plan, someone paraphrased a Henry David Thoreau quote to me, and it was a powerful reinforcement of everything Bernie had said: *"Of course you need to build your castles in the air. That's where they should be. Then you build your foundations under them."* The ideal scene was my castle in the air; by doing the business plan, I was making a blueprint that was the first step toward building that foundation.

Every successful business and career is based on a vision. Someone has first clearly imagined its development and growth long before that growth occurred in physical reality. I saw more clearly what Bernie had been telling me: What begins as a dream, a fantasy, an "ideal scene," must be translated into a solid business plan, with specific numbers. This sets in motion the forces that can bring the fantasy into concrete reality.

I WENT TO SEE BERNIE AGAIN a few weeks later, armed with a substantially revised plan. I was nervous about it; we were asking for a great deal more money than before. But given that amount of investment, the plan felt solid. There were enough reserves for any contingencies I could imagine. At least I hoped so. But then I've always been an optimist — though one with, at times, severe self-doubts.

Bernie met me at the door of his suite, wearing the same comfortable old suit as before, apparently, with the same gold cuff links and tie tack. We sat on the balcony in the same seats, and he ordered his ham sandwich on white bread and coffee with milk and sugar.

He glanced through the plan quickly, as he had before. He seemed to know exactly what he was looking for — he skimmed over most of it, then stopped and focused carefully on certain information.

"This is much better. Hmm..."

I felt anxious; I was sweating. If he invested in us, we could finally have some money to develop new products and to promote them in the way they should be promoted. We would be able to pay off our debts, without having to constantly field anxious phone calls about overdue bills. And we would finally be able to pay ourselves a regular salary, week after week. I could quit my other part-time job and focus on the business.

Bernie gave me one of his penetrating looks. He was assessing something again, something within me.

"What's your main purpose in all this?" he asked me.

"My main purpose?" That question surprised me. I certainly hadn't given it much thought. In fact I hadn't given it any thought at all. Fortunately Bernie gave me some time to reflect a bit.

"In doing this plan," he said, "in raising this money — hopefully — you have some kind of purpose. What is it? Do you want to make a ton of money? Do you want to retire in a mansion? Be honest, now."

I had no other choice. I couldn't face his gaze and lie to him. But he was asking a very difficult question.

"When I try to put my main purpose into words," I said, "it comes out sounding pretty hackneyed, or something. But I'd like to help people. I'd like to do something significant, something meaningful...something that makes a valuable contribution to people and maybe even helps the world in some way be a better place to live in..."

I paused, searching for words. Bernie was in no hurry. There was a silence.

"That's as close as I can come at the moment, I guess." It wasn't a very good statement of purpose. I'd forgotten what we had put in our mission statement at the beginning of the plan. But Bernie didn't seem too disappointed.

"Good," he said, "you're on the right track. You have to have a higher purpose than making money in a business. If you have a higher purpose, you marshal all kinds of forces behind you and within you that support you in reaching your goals. You get support from all kinds of places — some that you plan on, some that you can't possibly plan on. It's almost mystical — I think it *is* mystical — I've seen it happen over and over. If your purpose is just making money, you wither and die. You might even be successful, to some degree, but you're still unfulfilled, and you wither and die. I've seen that happen over and over, too.

"Money is essential in business, but it's secondary. Money is the lifeblood of the business, but the business has to have a higher purpose to survive and thrive.

"There are a lot of people who believe that the purpose of a business is to make money. I feel sorry for them. They have such a tough row to hoe. You sense it all the time, from the little guys who'll do anything to make a buck to all the big corporations whose leaders are always using phrases like 'maximizing shareholder value.' It leads to stupid business decisions that can have disastrous results for the company and the environment.

"That kind of thinking is just stupid — well, I should call it *ignorant* instead, because some very bright people believe this way. But they're ignorant, they don't understand the results of their actions.

"It's as ignorant as believing that the purpose of our lives here on earth is to keep blood pumping through our bodies. Sure, we need to have blood pumping through our bodies in order to be alive, but our purpose in life is something far greater, far more significant."

He looked back at the plan and flipped through it casually, glancing at random at different pages. It was nerve-racking. I knew he was giving me valuable advice, but it was hard to focus on it.

"Each of us is different," he said, looking back at me again, and stressing his words so that I had no choice but to listen, "and each of us has a unique purpose for living. Each of us has been given some unique talents and abilities to accomplish that purpose. There is something you can do, and something I can do, that no one else can do in quite the same way.

"We all have these natural gifts. Sometimes it's difficult for us to discover what they are — and sometimes it's because they're so obvious; it's so easy for us to perform in a certain way that we take it for granted and we don't value it, we don't realize what a gift it is.

"Each and every one of us should spend some time — however much time is necessary, and whenever necessary — to reflect on our purpose, and discover our purpose. Our purpose involves service of some kind, and love, always; it is something that contributes to humanity and to the planet.

"I'll give you one more hint about purpose. You might want to look at it this way: You have a primary purpose and a secondary purpose. The primary purpose is all about your *being*, every moment of the day. It's not a matter of doing or having. It's a matter of being. Your secondary purpose can include doing and having; your secondary purpose is your work in the world. Some call it the Great Work, with capital letters. It's the work we're here to do. It's our calling, which is the meaning of the word *vocation*. It's our mission, if you will.

"Our purpose is a sacred thing. I don't think it's something we should go around advertising. I don't even think — and this is just my opinion, of course — but I don't think we should even tell anyone else what our purpose is, except maybe our best friend, or business partner, or marriage partner. We should discover our purpose ourselves, and live it. Then, and only then, are we really successful, because then we become fulfilled in life."

There was a moment of silence.

"Do you know what I'm talking about?"

I nodded, but found no words to say. He gave me that look again. Then he held up the plan.

"I'll roll the dice with you," he said.

SUMMARY

- A well-written business plan brings the fantasy of your "ideal scene" down into concrete terms. Your plan is your most essential step, because it contains your vision of the future put into writing.

- Every successful business is based on a vision. Someone clearly imagined the development and growth of that business long before that growth occurred in physical reality.

- You have to have a higher purpose than making money in a business. If you have a higher purpose, you marshal all kinds of forces behind you and within you that support you in realizing your dreams.

- You have a unique purpose for living, and you have been given unique talents and abilities to accomplish that purpose. You need to reflect on your purpose, and discover it, in order to be truly successful.

- You have a primary purpose and a secondary purpose. The primary purpose is all about your *being*, every moment of the day. Your secondary purpose can include doing and having; your secondary purpose is your work in the world. Some call it the Great Work. It's the work we're here to do. It's our calling, which is the meaning of the word *vocation*. It's our mission, if you will.

- True success always involves personal fulfillment, and you are fulfilled only by living and working in harmony with your purpose in life. Your purpose involves service of some kind, and love, always; it is something that contributes to humanity and to the planet.

KEY FOUR

See the benefits within adversity,
the opportunities in your problems,
and keep picturing success.

I WENT BACK TO THE OFFICE in a state of shock, mingled with euphoria. Bernie had said he would talk to his lawyer and call us in a few days and "firm up the details."

For some reason I had thought that, before he made his decision, he would carefully study every part of the business plan, and question us about the nature of our business and about our projections and expenses. I had imagined him challenging our numbers, questioning what we assumed we would need to spend on salaries or on other expenses — manufacturing, promotion, taxes. There was none of that. He made his decision much faster than I had expected.

A few days later, he called and set up another meeting. "We'll go over the terms," he said, "and if everything is okay with you, I'll get the papers drawn up. You're going to have to set up a corporation. Do you have a lawyer?"

"Well, not really — but we can get one," I said.

"Don't worry about it. I'll have my lawyer draw it up. It won't cost that much — it's boilerplate stuff."

"Okay." I was assuming the cost to incorporate would come out of his investment — we certainly didn't have it in the bank. We had, as usual, nothing at all in the bank.

"Oh, the only other thing I need is a list of your assets. All three owners will have to pledge your assets as collateral."

I had no choice but to be honest. "Bernie, we have very few assets."

"Any of you own a house?"

"No."

"Well, just list whatever you have."

I didn't want him to have any kind of wrong impression. "I've got to warn you, Bernie — it's not much."

"Don't worry about it — but draw up a list anyway."

"Okay..."

THE RITUAL OF OUR NEXT MEETING was exactly the same as the others. I wondered if Bernie ever tired of ham on white bread. He didn't eat that much of it though, I noticed. He didn't even finish half of it.

"I came across a great new business plan the other day," he said, flashing his gold cuff links. "It's a company that turns garbage into energy — they take garbage and run it through this process and turn it into little blocks that burn like coal, only cleaner. What a great business! Can you imagine? They pay you for your raw materials!"

He said it with the enthusiasm of a child. He seemed to be immensely enjoying what he was doing.

"The owners of the company asked me if I planned to retire," he said, smiling broadly. "I said I don't believe in retirement. Retiring sounds like something they do to old horses, sending them to pasture. I'll never retire. If you're doing what you love to do, why quit?

"I've invested in quite a few companies — that's what I love to do. And I'll tell you, the people I've invested in who have failed all really love me, you know? And some of those that get successful end up resenting me."

At the time I didn't know what he meant. Later on, I understood.

"I wish you great success," Bernie went on, "and I sure hope you don't end up resenting me. Because here's what I'm prepared to offer: I'll loan you the money you need for the first nine months. After that, you'll probably need some additional capital, according to your plan. I'll introduce you to my banker, and maybe the bank can take over financing at that point. We want to get you a line of credit with a bank as soon as possible.

"The loan will be a seven-year note; you pay interest only for the first year — or maybe two, if you need to. Interest will be three points above prime. I'll have an option in the deal as well — an option to exchange 25 percent of the amount of the note you owe for 25 percent ownership of the company. I can exercise the option any time during the next three years; after three years, it expires. Okay?"

I felt in no position to argue with him. He was holding all the cards. Later on I realized that by taking 25 percent of the principal — the amount he loaned us — off the note in exchange for owning 25 percent of the company, he was in effect valuing the company to equal the amount of his loan — and that was, at the time, a generous valuation, several times the gross sales for that year.

"Oh, one more thing," Bernie said, almost as if he had nearly forgotten it. "Did you bring a list of your collateral?"

I reluctantly handed it to him.

He glanced at it and broke into a big grin. "You weren't kidding when you said you had no collateral," he said, almost laughing. He seemed to think our financial situation was humorous. And he seemed impressed, too, that we were honest and made no attempt to inflate our assets — but then, it's hard to inflate something that's nonexistent.

"I'll have my lawyer set up a corporation. You'll need to protect all these assets, after all." This was Bernie's idea of a joke. "He'll call you. It won't take long to set up."

I MET BERNIE A SHORT TIME LATER at the office of his lawyer, a man about Bernie's age — whatever that was — who was a great storyteller. He and Bernie both regaled me with stories for well over an hour. Neither seemed in any hurry to get to the point.

Their stories were fascinating — they had a great many

years of experience between them. They both obviously loved what they were doing and found great pleasure in entertaining a newcomer to the business world.

The most memorable story Bernie's lawyer told was about an old man from India who had come into his office. He was shabbily dressed; he looked like one of the street people who lived in the area. He asked the lawyer to set up a corporation, and gave him a battered, greasy check for five thousand dollars for the retainer to begin the work. The lawyer thought the old man was a wacko living out a fantasy, and he gave the check to an assistant to see if by any chance it was good. The manager of the bank said it was definitely good; in fact the man had a *fifty-million-dollar* personal line of credit with the bank. It turned out the old man imported vast quantities of American-grown food to India, buying by the railcarload. Though he dressed like a street person, he was immensely wealthy.

Bernie told a memorable story, too: "I used to own a hotel in Havana, back in the fifties," he said. "I was driving to work one day, and there was a skirmish in the street, right in front of me. The police had surrounded a youngster, a supporter of Castro, and were arresting him. I was so close to that kid I could see his eyes, clearly. And I saw this incredible determination and commitment. And I realized Castro was going to win; Batista could not survive against that kind of fierce support.

"I sold the hotel, immediately. And I told the other owners to sell, too. But they all said, 'No, Castro will never take over. And even if he does, he has promised us he'll leave the hotels alone.' I sold and left town. Within a year, all those owners had lost everything."

There was a lesson in that story, I thought: *Trust your instincts.*

THEY FINALLY FINISHED their storytelling, and Bernie's lawyer put his hand on the pile of legal documents.

"Okay — let's get down to it." He looked at me in depth, as if he were sizing me up in the same way Bernie often did. "Bernie's been very good to us over the years...."

I wasn't sure what he meant by that, exactly. I figured it probably meant Bernie worked with a pool of investors, including his lawyer.

"He has an eye for talent," he said, looking at me. I had a feeling he was not very impressed by me; I felt young and inexperienced.

The next half hour or so was spent going over the documents — loan papers and articles of incorporation. There were six stockholders in our newly formed corporation: the three investors we had promised some form of equity and the three founders. Bernie had worked out a formula, giving what seemed like a fair amount of stock to everyone, relative to their particular contribution. It seemed fair to me at the time — though later on, as the years passed, I have to admit I wished I had challenged him a bit and suggested somewhat different percentages. But at the time, I was in a strange state of shock and not thinking too clearly. And Bernie seemed supremely confident and comfortable, as if the deal was structured perfectly. So I just signed everything. As we finished, he leaned back in his chair and gazed wistfully into the unknown.

"Never forget: I'm investing in *you*. I'm not investing in your business plan, or your corporation. You can have the greatest plan in the world, you can have the best-capitalized corporation in the world, but if you don't have good people running it, you have nothing.

"I'm investing in your vision and integrity and good sense. It's up to you to keep the vision of the company so clear that everyone you work with can feel it — and it has to be a vision of growth and success. You've got to be able to clearly imagine how your company can quickly become profitable, and steadily grow, increasing those profits, just as you've outlined in your plan.

"Remember the advice I gave you — one of the best single pieces of advice I've ever heard: It's up to you to be able to see that within every problem is an opportunity. Never forget what Napoleon Hill said: *'For every adversity, there's an equal or greater benefit.'* That, in one sentence, is the key to visionary business. Life is always filled with problems, but it's filled with opportunities as well. Learn to spot the opportunities — the benefits, the gifts — that are there in every problem."

He stopped for a moment, then said, "I hope you don't mind me sitting here spouting all this advice."

"No, not at all," I said. I had been listening carefully, trying to remember as much as I could.

"Okay, here's another piece of advice I can give you:

Spend some time in solitude, every day if you can. Spend some time reviewing your goals, keeping your dreams fresh in your mind, and looking for the opportunities that are always in front of you. Keep focused on your plan — both on the long-term goals and on the very next step in front of you. Always keep moving ahead. It's just a matter of one small step after another.

"Keep picturing success. Don't dwell on any pictures of failure. No company should *ever* go into bankruptcy — it's a failure of the vision of the leaders of the company. If you can't imagine failure and bankruptcy, you can't possibly fail.

"A good manager can take *any* kind of business and turn it around and make it successful. A poor manager can take any kind of business and run it into the ground. I've seen it over and over. So have you, if you stop to think about it."

I thought about it. I had seen it.

"Your success will probably take a different route than you planned — that happens all the time. The trick is to make a clear plan, a clear path to success, but then to be flexible enough to change your plans continually as new problems and obstacles and opportunities arise. Your business might look totally different in five years than you imagine it will look. That's okay. You have to be flexible, and willing to do whatever it takes to reach your goals. We live in a changing world; if we learn to adapt to those changes, we can always reach our goals, somehow. If we resist those changes, we are fighting against the universe, and we'll always lose that battle."

Bernie's lawyer was enjoying the spiel. He smiled and nodded, silently cheering Bernie on. He obviously loved Bernie; you could feel his affection in the warmth of his eyes.

"It's really exciting to me every time we set up a new corporation," Bernie said. "The corporation is a great invention, when you think about it — as great an invention as compound interest, which was a brilliant invention. The corporation is its own legal entity; it's an individual, just like you and me. It grows like you and me. It goes through the stages of infancy, youth, and maturity. It takes on its own personality — reflecting its leaders in an almost mystical way — but it has a life of its own, separate from its owners or employees or anyone else.

"Every corporation, like every individual, has the capability to be infinitely creative. There are endless possibilities open to every corporation, just as there are to every individual."

He leaned forward in his chair and looked directly at me again. I felt like an awkward student in the presence of a master.

"For the company to stay healthy, and to grow, you always have to remember this: *The corporation is number one.* Put the interests of the company before your own interests, and before the interests of any owners, any employees, or anyone else.

"Never, never forget that. Take care of the corporation, first and foremost, and it will take care of you, and take care of all of its owners and employees and many others as well. But as soon as you place yourself — or anyone else, or the interests of any group — above the corporation, the business will suffer. And then everyone suffers. *Everyone.*"

He settled back into his chair, but still talked with intensity.

"Some people I knew a while ago — I knew them very well — had an experience we can all learn from. They had a family business, and it was very successful for many years. It had four owners — the children of the original founder, who'd passed on. They made a lot of money from the business; it was a cash cow for many, many years. Then it ran into some problems — the problems, of course, were the result of a lack of vision of the owners, because they became focused on the problems and lost sight of the opportunities.

"They ran into a recession, some of their products became obsolete, their procedures hadn't changed in years, and there were other problems as well. Again, there are opportunities there, even in recessions and in changes in society that make things obsolete. But they couldn't see the opportunities. They'd gotten too complacent; they weren't changing with the times. And they were spending a ton of money on overhead, on luxury offices and company cars, and they had a lot of employees who were pretty comfortable, and had been for years, and weren't working too hard. The business was still profitable, but far less profitable than it had been. So the owners needed to take less out of the company.

"Two of the owners were willing to take far less money — but the other two had not managed their money well and were overextended, with big mortgages, big family-support payments, all kinds of ongoing expenses. They'd gotten addicted to the high income level they'd enjoyed for many years, and they couldn't cut back. Their CPA told them they had to cut back or risk destroying the company — and they still couldn't cut back! They voted to continue drawing as much as ever out of the company.

"Do you see what they were doing? They put their own interests above the interests of the corporation — and they ended up killing the goose that was laying golden eggs for them, year after year. The whole thing collapsed in a nasty family fight — it was sad to see. It was painful. The only winners in the mess were the lawyers. They ended up liquidating and selling their assets for pennies on the dollar. They lost their company, and their steady stream of income, all because they didn't put the well-being of the company above their own interests.

"There's a lot to learn from this. One thing is this: Don't get overextended. When you have good years — and I hope you have many good years — use your profits to build up cash reserves, personally as well as in the business, so you have something to draw on during the lean years. But the most important thing is to *take care of the business first* — don't ever forget that."

"I won't." How could I? I had never seen Bernie so animated.

"Okay, I'm through preaching," he said, and he gestured broadly to the lawyer, as if he were handing him the stage. The lawyer handed me a large black three-ring binder, in a sheath, that contained all the articles of incorporation, by-laws, and stock certificates. Then he gave me the largest check I'd ever held in my hands.

SUMMARY

- To succeed, you have to have a vision of growth and success. You've got to be able to clearly imagine how your company can become profitable and steadily grow, increasing those profits, just as you've outlined in your plan.

- *"For every adversity, there is the seed of an equal or greater benefit."* Napoleon Hill, in that one sentence, gave us the key to visionary business. *In every problem there is an opportunity.* As was written in the Bhagavad Gita five thousand years ago, *"Even in the knocks of life, we can find great gifts."* That is a great key to success: Look for the benefits, opportunities, and even gifts in every problem you encounter.

- Spend some time in solitude, every day if you can. Review your goals, keep your dreams fresh in your mind, and look for the opportunities that are presenting themselves. Focus on your plan. Always keep moving ahead.

- Don't dwell on any pictures of failure; keep picturing success. No company should ever go into bankruptcy — it's a failure of the vision of the leaders of the company.

- A good manager can take any kind of business and turn it around and make it successful. A poor manager can take any kind of business and run it into the ground.

- Your success will probably take a different route than you planned. The trick is to make a clear plan, a clear path to success, but then to be flexible enough to change your plans continually as new problems and obstacles and opportunities arise.
- Remember: *The corporation is number one.* Put the interests of the corporation before your own interests and those of anyone else, and it will take care of you, and its owners and employees, and many others as well.
- The corporation is a brilliant invention, and within it, as within every individual, are infinite possibilities. A corporation can be used in endlessly creative ways. Your growth in business, as in life, is a never-ending process.

KEY FIVE

Plan your work and work your plan;
the employee handbook, benefits,
and profit sharing.

W̲E̲ ̲B̲A̲N̲K̲E̲D̲ ̲T̲H̲E̲ ̲C̲H̲E̲C̲K̲, and immediately started spending it. I worried about how quickly it was dwindling, but we were spending according to plan. When we received our first paychecks from our infant corporation, I was more concerned than elated; I worried that we might burn through our limited resources too quickly and those regular paychecks might not continue.

I realized, though, that these worries were not based on the kind of thinking Bernie was always encouraging, *visionary* thinking. I tried not to even imagine the worst-case scenarios that would come to mind; I tried to let them go as soon as I became aware of them. I tried the best I could to follow Bernie's advice and focus on the plan: the long-range

view, a year down the road, and the short-term steps we
needed to take to keep moving toward that long-range goal.

I attempted to save some money, but noticed how
quickly my lifestyle changed to accommodate my new
income level. It was a modest income, but certainly higher
than my previous one. I needed a car, a television — soon
I was quite accustomed to spending nearly all my paycheck.

I didn't forget Bernie's story about the people who lost
their business, though, and I arranged to have a modest
amount withdrawn from my checking account every month
and invested in a mutual fund. When and if my income
increased I vowed to increase the amount I invested regularly.

WE DIDN'T HEAR FROM BERNIE for over a month. Then
one afternoon he called and said, "Mind if I drop by?"

"C'mon over!" I said.

He was there in almost no time — he must have called
from somewhere close by. He strolled around and chatted
with everyone. He seemed pleased with what he saw. Then
we went into my little office in the back. He saw the business plan on my desk, on top of one of several piles of
papers. Perhaps he sensed that I hadn't opened it since the
day we incorporated.

"Have you heard the phrase, *Plan your work and work
your plan?*" he asked.

"No..."

"It's good advice. It's very important. You've used your
plan to raise capital — that's good. But now be sure to keep
working your plan. Don't just let it sit there and collect dust.

Keep revising it every three months, ideally — or at least every six months. Plug in your actual sales at the end of the period, and compare them with your projected sales. Same with expenses. Keep working your plan. Keep those goals fresh in your mind."

He stretched, as if he were comfortably at home, and then settled himself down into a chair.

"Good group of employees," he said. "Nice people. That's important. I always like to meet the owners, and ideally the employees, of any company I invest in — even if I'm just buying common stock. I like to meet them surreptitiously, so they don't know who I am. That's why I just wandered into your office — that's the best way to see what's going on.

"Do you have an employee handbook of any kind?"

"What's that?" I asked, a bit sheepishly. I had no idea.

"Something you should handle as soon as possible. Ideally, as soon as you have any employees at all. There are two reasons for an employee handbook: One is for your protection, and the other is for the good of the employees, which is for the good of the business, of course.

"The part that protects you is some legalese I'll have my lawyer draw up for you — again, it's boilerplate stuff; it won't cost much. It includes an agreement your employees sign when they're hired, and another agreement they sign when and if they leave the company — something they sign at the same time they get their severance check. Basically, the agreement says that they have received a copy of the employee handbook and they understand that their employment is

'at-will,' and that either your company or your employee
is free to terminate their employment at any time, with
or without cause. You also agree that any disputes will be
resolved by mediation, and then by arbitration, if necessary.

"This agreement protects you from lawsuits and helps
you avoid legal conflict. That's some valuable advice: *Avoid
legal conflict; find ways to solve problems without lawyers.*
Lawyers are paid to start fights — if it goes into the courts
it becomes a war, and a war is by definition a lose-lose
proposition. Nobody wins, except the lawyers. A smart,
conscious business owner has no need for lawsuits, or for
lawyers, except for peaceful purposes — advising on certain
things or going over contracts."

I had an impulse to ask him exactly what he meant by
"conscious," but he went on quickly, and for some reason I
didn't feel comfortable interrupting. Bernie was on a roll.

"Learn to settle all conflicts without using lawyers. If
you absolutely can't resolve it on your own, go to mediation. A good mediator can work with both sides to come
up with a win-win solution. It's far better than a lawsuit.

"You agree to mediate instead; if you can't resolve the
problem that way, go to arbitration. But only as a last resort
— I've never in my life had to go to arbitration. And I've
gone to mediation only once, and it was a great experience.

"Try to settle all conflicts yourself, in a way that values
and respects everyone involved. You'll live a lot longer and
prosper a lot more."

It sounded like Bernie was a fan of Spock in *Star Trek:*
"Live long and prosper."

"The other part of the employee handbook — the fun part — spells out all the employee benefits. Do you have any benefits you've given your employees yet — in writing?"

"Not in writing," I said. "None of them have been with us for very long...we've talked about paid vacations, and sick leave — we're calling them 'wellness days,' so they don't have to pretend to be sick to take them. I don't think we can afford health care yet, but we all want to set up something as soon as possible."

"Good," said Bernie. "The best thing for the health of the company — and for you too — is to offer the best benefit package possible. You aren't making much money yet — but you can start with a generous number of vacation and sick-leave days. I mean *wellness* days — I like that. Vacations don't really cost you much out of your pocket. And they generate a lot of goodwill. Give them their birthdays off, too, and a cash bonus for their birthday — even if at first it's so small it's almost just a token thing. They'll appreciate it, believe me.

"Give bonuses at Christmas, on their birthdays, and at the end of your fiscal year — even if at first they're small. Then visualize those bonuses growing larger and larger. Give them a bonus on the anniversary of the day they joined the company, too, with a little card or note thanking them for their contribution. They'll really appreciate that."

This sounded like a good idea.

"I saw a study that claimed that employees value acknowledgment and appreciation even more than cash bonuses. I don't really believe that, but it's important to acknowledge your employees regularly. Certainly acknowledgment *and* a cash bonus is the best thing you can do.

"Get health insurance as soon as you can. Everybody needs health insurance these days — medical costs are ridiculous, astronomical. As soon as you're profitable, get a dental plan, too — those are actually fairly reasonable in terms of cost, and they're great to have. Most people use their dental plan a lot more than their medical plan.

"Every company should be able to provide medical and dental coverage for their people, without it costing the employees anything. If they can't, something is seriously wrong with their business model in the first place. It's sad when I hear business owners whining that they can't afford to pay medical benefits for their employees, whether the company's large or small. If they can't afford it, they're doing something wrong, because medical coverage doesn't cost that much — it's a minor part of an employee's salary."

On occasion, I'd had similar ideas about medical benefits. It felt wonderful to have someone as experienced as Bernie verify my feelings.

"And a pension plan is really important — have you looked into that?"

"Not really," I said. "We definitely want to do something in the future, but we haven't given it much thought."

"There are some great pension plans that are based on your profits — if you don't make a profit, you don't fund the plan. So it doesn't hurt the company in the bad years. But you can contribute out of your profits up to 10 or 15 percent of an employee's salary into a tax-sheltered plan. It builds over the years, and they have something substantial for retirement. And they can even borrow against it, for housing, education, and medical emergencies. And the employees don't have to put any of their own money into it. I'd look into it right away, and present it to your employees, as soon as possible, even before you're profitable. That gets everyone motivated to cut costs and increase sales and help make a profit. It gets everyone thinking like an owner.

"The cash bonuses I mentioned are the other important thing. Let me tell you a story — do you have any coffee?"

"Oh, yeah, Bernie, sorry!" I got up, embarrassed that I had been so inconsiderate. "Do you want anything else?"

"No, I'm fine — have you got sugar?"

A FEW MINUTES LATER, we settled down with a fresh cup of coffee, and Bernie told his story.

"Years ago I was in the hotel business, and I got an offer to manage a hotel in Switzerland. This was way before you were born, back in the last ice age. I went to Switzerland and toured the hotel — it was a mess, literally. The building was a wreck. It was losing money. Employee morale was horrible. Service was bad. There was a lot of what they call 'shrinkage' today: shrinkage — that cracks me up! It's a — what do you call it? — a euphemism for *theft*. Silverware, towels, toiletries, food, paint — you name it — kept disappearing. The employees were paid on the bottom end of the pay scale, and had no kind of pension plan or profit sharing, almost no benefits at all. The management-employee rapport was terrible, just a lot of resentment.

Employee turnover was really high, which costs a company a lot more than most bean counters seem to realize.

"I went to a meeting with all the owners, all the stockholders of the hotel. We sat around a big oval table — there must have been about twenty people there. I told them I'd accept the job on one condition — they would have to agree to raise wages and have a great benefit package for employees. They'd also have to agree to a formula I would implement, a simple formula: One-third of the profits would be plowed back into the hotel, one-third given to the employees as a cash bonus, and one-third would go to the shareholders.

"You should've seen their reaction! They looked like they thought I had lost my mind! They didn't mind plowing money back into the hotel, but the idea of paying the employees as much of the profits as the owners really got them worked up.

"I told them if they wanted me for the job, those were my terms. It was not negotiable. Besides, I pointed out, they weren't making any money anyway! The place was losing money! Lots of money! Isn't it a lot better to get 33 percent of something than 100 percent of nothing?

"They ended up hiring me for the job — I think they were desperate. The first thing I did was get all the employees together and tell them about the profit-sharing program. They would get one-third of the profits — as much as the owners were getting.

"You wouldn't believe the change in morale — well, I bet you would, come to think of it. The service improved *immediately.* And employee theft dropped to almost zero. The employees were thinking like owners, knowing they were going to get a good piece of the profits.

"After my first year there, the employees got a check out of the profits equal to about two weeks' pay. A few of the stockholders were still whining about the arrangement, but we had turned the business around and made it profitable. I left after seven years, and at the end of that time the employees' profit-sharing bonus was equivalent to over *eight months'* pay. In cash. Stockholders were happy. Employees were *ecstatic.* The guests were happy. The hotel looked great. It was a win-win-win-win situation."

He reached for his coffee with his long, delicate fingers.

"That's impressive, Bernie."

"Yeah, I did pretty well in the deal, too. They gave me stock in the company, and I got profits both as an employee and as a shareholder.

"So I recommend that you set up something similar. The percentage may be different in terms of what you have to retain in the company — a third of the profits may be more than you need to retain. But, above and beyond what you plow back into the company, I recommend you split whatever's left over fifty-fifty between owners and employees. Of course, any owners who are also employees get paid out of the employees' pot as well as the owners' pot, because they're fulfilling two separate roles. Owners deserve to be well paid for their investment or energy or vision or whatever it was that got them into that position. But employees deserve to be well paid, too, out of the profits of the company.

"Here's what I firmly believe, and my experience has borne it out — in fact, it's a self-fulfilling truth: *Give away half your profits to employees, and the company will make over twice the profit it was making.* It'll do so well that, in the long run, you'll make much more as an owner than if you had kept all the profits. It's win-win profit sharing.

"*All* businesses should have profit sharing, even the tiniest little mom-and-pop operations. Profit sharing that includes *everyone.* There's no excuse for not doing it — it just makes good business sense: In the long run, owners will make more money if they share profits generously with everybody, even part-time workers.

"Even the smallest company — say one with a single, part-time employee — could set up something. Just say to your people, 'Look, we're going to give you some of the profits. We don't know how much; we don't know if we'll be profitable or not. But if we are, you'll see a share of it.' Then watch what happens."

I had been thinking that profit sharing was something we would do later, once we were profitable. Now Bernie was showing me how we could set it up even before we were profitable. I made a mental note to talk to everyone about it.

"Every business should set up profit sharing," Bernie said. "I'd like to see the post office set up profit sharing. Can you imagine? Run it like a private business and share the profits. McDonald's should set up profit sharing, and get their employees off that ridiculously low minimum wage, too. How can anyone live on minimum wages these days, and keep a roof over their heads? It's a mystery to me. I'd even pay more for a Big Mac if I knew they paid higher than minimum-wage salaries and had profit sharing.

"What if the *government* had profit sharing? Think of that! There's certainly some creative way to set it up — the government's just a business — a huge business, with way too many agencies and special interests, but it's a business nonetheless. All the different offices could have different goals — especially cost-cutting goals. If the managers and employees cut, say, 20 percent of their costs, they get a 5 percent bonus. Something like that. There are all kinds of things that could be done, if they'd be motivated to think creatively — and that's what profit sharing does.

"Giving employees bonuses for money-saving ideas is another great way to share profits. I've done that many times over the years.

"Your employees are your greatest asset. You can have the greatest products and services in the world, but if you don't have good employees creating those products and doing those services and selling and marketing your products and services, and handling your accounting and keeping expenses down and managing cash flow, you've got no business — you've got a series of severe headaches.

"So give your employees great benefits as soon as you are able to — *especially profit sharing*. You know what profit sharing does, bottom line? It instills pride of ownership in employees. After all, what is ownership in a business — what does it mean? It primarily means you get a share in the profits when the business is successful. It can also mean you get some kind of say in how the business is managed —

though not always. But as an owner, you're an idiot if you don't give employees a say in how the business is managed — they're in the trenches all day, doing their job, and they can see far more clearly than you can what the details and frustrations of that job are. They can usually see how to improve their performance better than you can — not always, but often. They have a perspective you don't have. So if you encourage them to think like managers, and pay them like owners, you give them pride of ownership. You give them job satisfaction. And they'll work hard for you, believe me. I've seen it happen over and over."

Bernie was animated, and it wasn't just because of the coffee. His spirit was inflamed with his ideas. I grabbed a notebook and started making notes.

"Treat your employees like responsible adults, treat them like valuable assets, and they'll act like responsible adults, and they'll become valuable assets. Through cash bonuses and building a pension plan, all of the employees who stay with you over time amass wealth and build for an abundant future. Call it the Get Rich Slowly with Marc Program, or whatever you want to call it. You can probably come up with a better name than that." He seemed amused with himself.

"Your ideas are very generous," I said.

"Some people have accused me of being too generous — 'generous to a fault' — but I look at it this way: I'm generous for my own selfish purposes, because I am far more successful because of my generosity. I know how to create

long-term win-win relationships, and that's the key to success in this world.

"And besides, it's far better to be too generous than too
stingy; it's better to give too much vacation time than not
enough; it's better to give too many perks than not enough;
it's better to be too easygoing than too driven; and it's far
better to be too forgiving than too judgmental."

He smiled broadly and reached for the dregs of his sug-
ary coffee. It occurred to me that when someone is speaking
the truth, everyone knows it's the truth because it's obvious.
As the founders of our country said, truth is *self-evident*.

Bernie went on: "The business is a vehicle to realize your
dreams. Work with all your employees so they can realize
their dreams as well — whether their dreams lie through
continued work with the company or eventually outside it.
Have them all do a five-year plan, unless they don't feel
comfortable doing that — some people have difficulty projecting that far in advance. But work with them to help
them imagine their future, in the same way I encourage you
to work on your future. It's a win-win situation for you and
your employees. Not only does it help them realize their
dreams, but it engenders friendship and loyalty. It makes
them know they're a vital part of the team."

He sat quietly for a moment, looking a little like Yoda
once again.

"Oh, one more little piece of advice, and then I'll go.
This is something that should be obvious to every supervi-
sor and employer, but it isn't: When you praise an employee

— and you should praise them as much as possible —
praise them publicly, in front of others. When you have to
criticize them, or correct their work in any way, do it in private. This is a simple key to good management, one that
should be taught to everyone, including every parent and
everyone in a serious relationship."

I scribbled several pages of notes after Bernie left. I felt
like heading it, "The Gospel According to Bernie."

SUMMARY

- Plan your work and work your plan. Keep revising your business plan, putting in actual sales figures and comparing them with what you had projected. Keep your goals fresh in your mind.
- Create an employee handbook that protects you as an employer from spurious lawsuits and spells out a generous package of benefits for each employee.
- Avoid legal conflict. Find ways to solve problems without lawyers. A conscious business owner has no need for lawyers, except for peaceful purposes.
- Every company — large or small — should have generous paid vacations, medical and dental insurance, a pension plan, and profit sharing.
- Give away half your profits — after retaining what you need to retain in the company — to your employees, and the company will do so well that, in the long run, the owners will make much more than if they had kept all the profits. This is win-win profit sharing.
- Through profit sharing and a pension plan, every employee that stays with the company can, over time, amass wealth and build for an abundant future.
- Praise employees publicly. Correct their work in private.

- It is far better to be too generous than too stingy; it is better to give too many perks than not enough; better to be too easygoing than too driven; and far better to be too forgiving than too judgmental.

KEY SIX

Avoid management by crisis;
make a clear annual goal.

I TOOK BERNIE OUT TO LUNCH a few weeks later; it was the first time our little company picked up the tab. It wasn't a large tab; Bernie was happy to eat in a hamburger joint with formica-topped tables. He was happy to eat anywhere that served ham sandwiches on white bread.

I told him about our latest projects; he seemed interested, not so much in the projects themselves, but in what they would cost and what we projected they would do in sales. We had come up with a "feasibility study" for each project: Our marketing director projected the first year of sales, and our financial department — our part-time bookkeeper and I — projected expenses and profits. Bernie seemed impressed.

"You seem to be going after projects, making them happen," he said. "That's important. Don't just sit back and wait for great things to fall in your lap. Decide what you want and go out there and get it. Do you have a clear goal of the sales you want to have for the year?"

The question caught me a little off guard; I hesitated for a moment. It was in the business plan, but it didn't come to mind right away.

"That number should be right on your tongue," Bernie said. "It should be *emblazoned* in your mind. Write it down and stick it in front of your face. Put it on your desk, put it in your billfold with your money. Put it anywhere that will remind you, and keep it in mind. Write it on your bathroom mirror, do anything you need to do to get it deeply into your subconscious mind. Keep telling your subconscious your sales and your profits for the year, and your subconscious will show you exactly how to get there. That's how powerful your subconscious is!

"I read a very interesting thing in the paper a while ago. A company was struggling, and some of the managers of a certain division bought the division from the parent company and spun it off as an independent company. It was doing something like four million a year in sales, and was losing money. The managers went to the employees with a plan to achieve something like 34.23 million in sales in five years. Their plan precisely spelled out what they needed to do to reach that exact goal of 34.23 million in annual sales in five years.

"And you know what? They nailed it right on the head,

exactly 34.23 million dollars. That shows you the power of a detailed plan, and a clearly defined, specific goal.

"*Keep your mind focused on your goal.* Don't let doubts, fears, and 'small thinking' undermine your goal. Don't think too small — if you do, the company you create will always remain small. Your company reflects your mind; it reflects your dominant visualization."

I couldn't help smiling; hearing this old man with slicked-back white hair using the word *visualization* once again seemed somehow incongruous. I agreed with what he was saying, though. And he backed up his theories with a lot of experience. He continued on, unconcerned about my responses to his words.

"If you can hold a vision of your company as successful, profitable — with specific numbers, always growing — your company will continue to grow and succeed. But if you keep focusing on all the difficulties involved in growth, all the problems in the day-to-day operations of the company, personality disputes, problems with getting new products out and with suppliers and distributors and cash flow and so on and so on, you'll end up creating nothing but problems and getting nowhere.

"But if you keep focused on a vision of your success, if you keep a clear picture in your mind of where you want to be a year from now, and even five years from now — if you can do that — you'll end up aligning the exact forces you need to bring about your success. *Keep focused on a clear goal, and the universe will work out the details.*"

That phrase had an impact — I wouldn't forget that

phrase! Could it really be that simple — if you keep focused on a goal, the universe would work out the details? Bernie went on, speaking with absolute confidence, as if everything he said was the obvious truth.

"Only you can create your success, and only you can block your success. If your visualization of success is stronger than your doubts and fears, you'll succeed. It's that simple. If you let your doubts and fears overwhelm you, those doubts and fears will undermine your success. You'll end up creating what you doubt and fear rather than what you desire.

"You've got to keep the big picture in mind, and keep assuring yourself that you can achieve the big picture. You've got to be your own coach, and your own cheerleader."

A waiter came by. "Okay, I'll have another cup of coffee," Bernie said. "This is definitely a two-cup conversation." He beamed with enthusiasm, and even sounded a little like a coach and a cheerleader.

"Richard Bach once said — I think it was in *Illusions* — 'argue for your limitations, and they are yours.' When you argue for your limitations, you always win the argument. If you keep thinking *it's so hard to succeed*, then it's very difficult for you to succeed.

"Success follows a line of thinking that is focused on success. Failure follows a line of thinking dominated by doubts and fears. Your dominant thinking will always prove itself to be true. It cannot be otherwise. It is a law of nature. All thought becomes self-fulfilling."

He sipped on his coffee. I hoped I could remember his words.

"There are just two styles of management, as far as I'm concerned: management by crisis and management by goals. The people who are caught in the management-by-crisis trap get so focused on the day-to-day problems that they never have time to step back and see the big picture. They're always working *in* the business and never have time to work *on* the business. The day-to-day details become all-consuming, and their vision of the future is lost. They probably had some kind of vision in the first place, some kind of dream, but all their anxieties around day-to-day problems have eroded the dream, and finally destroyed it. It has no power anymore. It's been forgotten.

"A dream is a fragile thing — yet it can be the most powerful thing in the world. But it needs to be constantly reinforced, so that it becomes firmly rooted in the subconscious. When that dream is put down in a concrete, achievable plan, on paper, then the magic happens: All kinds of forces you never dreamed of come into play and help you manifest your dream.

"I definitely believe it's a form of magic — and I've seen it happen over and over in my life.

"God, I get to talking so much I forget to eat."

I felt a wave of affection for Bernie as he picked up his ham sandwich. The guy was more than a businessman — he was a magician. He understood visualization. He understood magic. And he used his power to create a great deal of good in the world.

SUMMARY

- Have a clear goal of the sales and profits you want to achieve for the year *emblazoned* in your mind.

- Don't let doubts, fears, and "small thinking" undermine your goal. Don't think too small — if you do, the company you create will always remain small. Your company reflects your mind; it reflects your dominant visualization.

- There are just two styles of management: management by crisis and management by goals. Those caught in the management-by-crisis trap are always working *in* the business and never have time to work *on* the business. Their vision of the future is lost.

- If you keep a clear picture in your mind of where you want to be one year from now, you'll end up aligning the exact forces you need to bring about your success. The universe will work out the details.

- A dream is a fragile thing, yet it can be the most powerful thing in the world. But it needs to be constantly reinforced so that it becomes firmly rooted in the subconscious, and it needs to be supported by a concrete, achievable plan. Then the magic happens: All kinds of forces come into play and help you manifest your dream.

KEY SEVEN

Give abundantly and reap the rewards.

W E WALKED BACK TO THE OFFICE taking a longer, more scenic route along the edge of a park. We needed a bit of exercise after that lunch.

"This is a beautiful part of the world," Bernie said. "And it hasn't been destroyed by mindless industry."

It was surprising to hear such a probusiness person talk of "mindless industry," but then Bernie was full of surprises.

"It's a crying shame the way business has polluted so much of the planet," he said. "And it's all their fault. They have no one else to blame. It's the managers of the corporations, who think that the most important thing in the world is the amount of money they make for shareholders — and for themselves, of course. And that's *not* the most important thing — it is important, but there are far more important things, like the quality of life for all of us on this beautiful, fragile planet of ours."

I couldn't help but smile as this old man in a brown suit with his flashy gold cuff links and tie tack talked about our beautiful, fragile planet.

"People and the planet are far more important than profits, in the long run." That was Bernie's version of the triple bottom line.

"Let me say this about business ownership. With ownership comes responsibility. Whatever you own — whether it's a car, a house, or a business — you're responsible for it. You're responsible for maintaining it, and you're responsible for its impact in the world.

"You have to maintain your house, or it loses its value. You have to maintain your car so it doesn't pollute too much — that's the law. And business owners have a responsibility to maintain their businesses, which most of them think means to make them grow and make them more and more profitable. And that's important. But there are other aspects of ownership a lot of owners just don't see — or don't care to think about — and their blindness, their lack of vision, creates a lot of problems in the world.

"The owners of a business have a great responsibility toward their employees, and their communities, and the environment. Just as they want to create happy and healthy lives for themselves, owners are *responsible* for creating healthy and happy lives for their employees.

"This is where a lot of companies — large and small — blow it. Those large manufacturers who move their operations offshore so they can pay their employees dirt-poor wages and pollute the environment are asking for major trouble down the line. They put profits first and foremost and ignore everything else. Their workers suffer in poverty. They pollute the environment.

"What they have to realize is that they're responsible for the welfare of their employees, and the environment too. Ownership has a responsibility to these things as well as to the bottom line. In the long run, supporting employees and the local community and helping the environment heal again is good for business, even good for the bottom line.

"Henry Ford understood about paying employees well: He paid his workers far more than he could have, and when he was asked why, he said he needed to pay them well because he needed them to be able to buy his cars. That makes great sense. Pay your people well, and they'll have money to spend. It's good for the whole economy, which is good for your business, and every other business."

We walked in silence for a while. Then he shook his head sadly and went on.

"This kind of mindless, amoral ownership — or, in many cases, immoral ownership — that's so prevalent today is the main cause of pollution, and a major cause of poverty as well. Pollution and poverty mean a decline in the quality of life for all of us, because we're all in this boat together."

He stopped and gazed into the park. His eyes had that Yoda-like look of sadness and humor.

"So take care of your people and take care of your environment, even if your bottom line is a little less spectacular as a result, at least in the short run. It's money well spent. If you can't run a business without exploiting people or polluting the planet, you shouldn't be in that business in the first place. Or else you need to reinvent your business model so you take care of the triple bottom line: *people, planet, and profits.*

"That phrase is catching on more widely now — thank God! People and the planet are as important — in fact, more important — than profits.

"I don't care what any CEOs may claim: *Every* business, every industry, has a responsibility to take care of its employees and to help the local communities where they have their plants and offices.

"And every business, every industry, has a responsibility to minimize pollution. We're all responsible for cleaning up the mess we've made. And we should do it, without excuses, without procrastinating.

"Look at the auto business — a major contributor to worldwide pollution. Henry Ford knew he could build a car that burned a relatively clean fuel, but his old friend Rockefeller talked him out of it, because Rockefeller was in the oil business. I'll bet you if they could have had the foresight to see the pollution that decision created, they would have gotten into cleaner fuels, and this world would be a healthier place to live in. The auto companies have a major challenge ahead of them. They should quit procrastinating and create vehicles that burn clean fuels."

He looked for a moment like an old King Lear, raging at the storm.

"What can you and I do about it? A lot. We can put in solar power and run as green a business as possible. We can certainly make our views known to the powers that be. And here's something you can do that will have a global impact: As soon as you start making a profit, give a generous percentage of that profit to organizations working to improve the world in some way, locally or globally. Donate generously, both through your company and as an individual.

"*Every* corporation should donate generously. If every profitable business in the world gave even just 5 percent of their profits to nonprofit corporations that are working to help people and the environment, think of the impact that would have!

"Shareholders would certainly continue to survive — and thrive — with 5 percent of their profits going to good causes rather than into their pockets. And that amount of money would have incredible impact! If half of the individuals on earth and half of the corporations donated even 5 percent of their income, we could end starvation around the world, house the homeless, have free education, from preschool to college, and clean up the whole planet.

"A writer named Charles Colton put it beautifully, '*If universal charity prevailed, Earth would be a heaven, and Hell a fable.*'

"There's a lot we can all do. Start where you can, and do

what you can. It'll all come back to you, believe me, in more ways than one — including financially. Tell the world you're a green company, and you donate 5 percent of your profits, and you'll find more and more people who will choose to do business with you just because they know that their money is doing some good in the world. It's just good business — the kind of practices we need to survive and thrive in the future."

These words came to mind, but I didn't feel comfortable expressing them: *Bernie, you're a visionary.*

We came up to his car — a brand-new Cadillac. I wondered if there was any contradiction between Bernie's pro-environmental talk and his choice of automobiles. I hoped there wasn't. Bernie deserved to ride in comfort and safety. He opened his door, hesitated, then said, "Do you have time for a story?"

"Sure."

"Let's walk around the block again. It's good to get some exercise."

"There's a nice little park over there, Bernie."

"Yeah," he said. "Let's take a stroll in the park."

We spent the next half hour or so in light conversation. Bernie admired the trees and the flowers, and could identify most of them. He stopped at one point to smell the roses in somebody's front yard. He told about the birds nesting in the eaves of his house. The young ones occasionally fell out of their nest, and Bernie and his wife would keep the cats away while they got a ladder and put the baby birds back in their nests. I could just see Bernie climbing a ladder, probably in his brown suit, risking his old limbs to protect a fledgling bird. Then it occurred to me that he was guarding our little fledgling company in the same way.

He finally got to his story.

"I'll never forget one of my first jobs, right out of high school," he said. "It was a small business, a very successful one. I did grunt work; I did a bit of everything. The owner made a lot of money — I mean, he was making a *fortune*. But he paid his people as little as possible, gave us no benefits at all, and tried to get the absolutely cheapest deal from every supplier he dealt with. He felt the more money he could squeeze out of his suppliers and employees meant the more money he would put in his pocket. And he was right — for a while. He ended up making a great deal of money, *for a while*.

"But he was really stupid in the long run — he didn't know, he didn't understand that a person's quality of life is far more valuable than their bank balance — and the quality of his life was absolutely miserable. He had a constant battle with his employees: They were always leaving for greener pastures. Turnover was horrible. He paid them no severance pay or anything, of course, so they'd just walk out the door when they got mad at him and leave the place in chaos.

"He was in a constant state of stress because someone had left, and he had to cover in an emergency situation. There was one crisis after another, continuously. He always had troubles with his suppliers, because he always pressured them to give him more for less money. He was never able to enjoy his money — he was too busy working — and he died far too young of a heart attack while fighting a nasty lawsuit. So, in the long run, he ended up making far less money than he could have, because the stress killed him when he should have had many good years left.

"I despised him when I worked for him — everyone did — but I feel sorry for him now. He lacked understanding. He had no wisdom, no vision. Everyone I ever worked for taught me a great deal, but that man taught me more than anyone else. He taught me that the quality of our lives is much more important than the amount of money we make. The stress he created for himself was not worth all the riches in the world. He died far too young, alone and miserable. His wealth was worthless to him.

"He didn't understand the law of giving and receiving. I'm convinced there's a special kind of hell — and it's right here on earth — for those who understand the principles of success well enough to amass wealth, but don't understand those principles well enough to be able to give to others.

"That was his fatal flaw — he couldn't give. He never supported anyone. Not even his own children, or his ex-wives. And certainly not his employees. He never understood that successful businesses, and successful relationships in general, are built on *service to others*.

"I agree with Andrew Carnegie: I see no value whatsoever in amassing large quantities of money — the money simply becomes something that corrupts and weakens future generations. It's far better to give! Give your money away!

"I think it's *sick* that so many rich people are sitting on tens of millions, hundreds of millions — and *billions* — of dollars. Think of the good they could do with that money! Think of the number of homeless people they could house and feed, or the ways they could help their local communities. Think of the support they could give to nonprofits doing so much good work globally. Think of the positive environmental impact they could have!

"How much does one person need? That's a good question. A million? Ten million? Fifty million? Fine. Give the rest away — give some of it to your family, fine — support them in living the life of their dreams. But give the rest of it away! Circulate that wealth.

"Private businesspeople have done a lot of good for the world, but they could do so much more. Look at that guy who's guaranteeing college educations for a thousand inner-city kids, and who rebuilt their youth center! Did you hear about him?"

I nodded; I had just read about him in the paper.

"Look at the good he's doing with his money! If we could encourage more private citizens to act the way he's acting, we could solve the problems of the world.

"Look at what Bill Gates and Warren Buffett are doing with their wealth — I'm sure this is influencing a lot of rich people. They've realized that when you pass billions of dollars on to your heirs, it just messes them up. As Buffett put it, 'You should give them enough to support them in their dreams, but not so much that they don't have to do anything.'

"Gates and Buffett are leaving their families just a tiny fraction of their wealth, and putting the rest into nonprofit foundations to improve the world.

"*Every* wealthy person should do that. Ted Turner said something very perceptive: He said the *Forbes Magazine* list of the four hundred wealthiest people in the world was far too widely admired. He said the people on it, or who want to be on it, are all very competitive, and to get on that list you've got to retain your wealth. It would be far better, he said, to focus our competitive spirit on the list of people who give away the most each year — the biggest donors. That would be far better for everyone in the whole world."

I chuckled. It was fun to see Bernie so animated.

"Start with your own employees, and take care of them. Then find some worthy causes to support, in your local community and globally as well. Ultimately, it's for our own self-interest.

"We all have our own self-interest at heart — and that's as it should be. Each one of us has unique strengths, and a unique contribution to make to the world. Keeping our own self-interest in mind is absolutely necessary for us to realize our potential, our purpose in life.

"But people who have even just a little bit of wisdom understand that they can reach their goals only by serving others as best as they can, and helping others achieve *their* goals. It's a wonderful system: I scratch your back, you scratch mine. I can't scratch my own back very well; it's much more pleasurable to have someone else do it — and it's fun to give someone else the pleasure of having their back scratched.

"That old boss of mine probably didn't know he was a great teacher, in spite of himself. He taught me a great deal. He taught me how not to run a business, and that's important. He taught me the value of priorities. Money is not the final measure of a person's worth — there are far more important things: the kind of life we lead; the way we treat others, and our communities and environment; the service we do for others; the amount of love and compassion we have for others; our contribution to others and to our planet. That's what is important in life. That's the measure of a person's worth.

"The most important words to remember and try to practice, in business and in life, are *love, compassion, tolerance*, and *generosity* — for yourself and for others. Remember to love and serve yourself and others. Let those words guide you, and you'll never go wrong."

We walked back to his car in silence; his words were words to ponder.

- As owner of your business, you have a responsibility to your employees, your community, and your environment.

- In the long run, supporting employees and your community and helping the environment heal is good for business, good for the bottom line. If you can't run a business without exploiting people or polluting the planet, you shouldn't be in that business in the first place, or else you need to reinvent your business model. Remember the triple bottom line: *people, planet, and profits*. And remember that, in the long run, people and planet are far more important than profits.

- Give a generous percentage of your profits to organizations working to improve the world. It will all come back to you, in more ways than one.

- The quality of our lives is far more important than the amount of money we make. And there is no value whatsoever in amassing large quantities of money. It is far better to give it away! Corporations and private businesspeople could do so much more to help people and heal the environment.

- Successful businesses, and successful relationships in general, are built on service to others. You can reach your goals only by serving others as best as you can, helping others achieve their goals.

- Money is not the final measure of a person's worth — there are far more important things: the kind of life you lead; the way you treat others, your communities, and the environment; the service you do for others; the amount of love and compassion you have for others; your contribution to others and to your planet.

- The most important words to remember and to try to practice, in business as well as in life in general, are *love, compassion, tolerance,* and *generosity* — for yourself and for others. Love and serve yourself and others — let those words guide you, and you'll never go wrong.

KEY EIGHT

"Love change, learn to dance,
and leave J. Edgar Hoover behind."

SEVERAL MONTHS PASSED QUICKLY. The time seemed
to fly by much faster now that I was working full-time for
myself. I'd glance at the clock and be surprised it was so late.
Sometimes I'd have a wave of panic and think there just
weren't enough hours in the day — there just wasn't enough
time to do all the diddly details that needed to be done. But
then I'd think of Bernie, and how relaxed he seemed to be
all the time, and how he always had time for a story or two.
Somehow that was reassuring to me; I just needed to do as
much as I could each day and leave the rest for later.

We didn't hear from Bernie for several months. Then
one morning, our new receptionist buzzed me in my office
on our new phone system.

"There's someone called Burtie or something who wants to talk to you."

"Burtie? Did he say Bernie?"

"Ahh . . . he might have. I'm not sure."

It was Bernie, all right.

"New receptionist, huh?" he said.

"Well, she's been here a few months, but . . . there's a lot to learn."

"Yeah, the receptionist has to know what's going on. It's a very important job, because it's the first contact anyone has with the company. I wouldn't expect her to know who I was — but be sure she knows your main people, and knows what's going on in general."

Bernie was being modest — the receptionist should have known about him, and we both knew it. I made a mental note to spend some time with her and fill her in on all the different people we regularly had contact with.

"Do you want to meet for lunch or something, later in the week?" he asked. "It's been over six months already — do you have a report for me?"

"Sure thing," I said, stretching the truth a bit. Well, I told myself, I'd have it by the time I saw him.

I WENT UP TO BERNIE'S HOTEL ROOM and found him sitting out on the balcony as usual, overlooking the lobby. He was doing nothing, apparently, except watching the show below. People were scurrying around while we sat like some gods in the mythic past, looking down on humanity from our lofty perch. Bernie relaxed and sipped his coffee.

I handed him a copy of our report, and he glanced through it for a few minutes. We hadn't reached the sales we had hoped for, but we were getting close. And some unexpected expenses had come up, like the need for a new phone system. I was certainly glad we had added an additional 15 percent for contingencies, as Bernie had told us to. If we hadn't done that, we would have been in trouble.

"This is a good report," Bernie said. "You're planning your work, and working your plan. Keep revising this baby — don't get complacent. Your ship has to have a course."

I told Bernie the business didn't feel like a ship to me — it felt more like a big old barge that was just sitting there at the dock, going nowhere. It felt like we were little tugboats, pushing and pushing the barge, and the barge wasn't moving at all.

"That's interesting," Bernie said. "Those almost visual images we have are very important, very powerful, because they come directly from your subconscious, and reflect your image of the business. You believe your company is *stuck*. You've got to change that image.

"If you see it as a barge, so be it — but start to imagine that barge is moving, slowly at first perhaps, but moving. Then watch it gain momentum, and move with its own power, so you won't need your little tugboats. Watch it cruise through the water, with you carried along on it, completely supported by it. Imagine yourself enjoying a great ride!

"I tell you, as soon as you can change your mental concept of it — your visualization of it — the business will change. Your *life* will change."

His words reminded me of a phrase I'd heard from Henry Ford: *"If you think you can, or if you think you can't, you're right."*

BERNIE'S HAM SANDWICH on white bread arrived from room service.

"Ooh . . . thanks for this! It looks *scrumptious*. My compliments to the chef." Was Bernie flirting with the waitress? He watched her walk away, an appreciative smile on his face.

"I heard a fascinating thing on the radio the other day," he said. "It was about the CEO of Pepsico — I didn't catch his name, but I've heard it before. Anyway, in his five years with the company, profits have been up 30 percent per year, every year.

"He said his success is due to the fact that they follow three rules. They're easy to remember, very creative. His three rules are love change, learn to dance, and leave J. Edgar Hoover behind."

I guess I gave him a quizzical look.

"The first rule is obvious: *Learn to accept change, even to love change.* The nature of life is change, and we either learn to love it, or resist the inevitable. Every company, like every person, is changing all the time. The world is changing all the time. Technologies change. People's tastes change. Their needs and desires change. Some companies have the vision to use that to their advantage; some don't. Those that don't, don't survive very long.

"A hundred years ago, selling buggy whips was a big, big business. But times change. Those who thought they were in the buggy whip business are out of business. Those who realized they were in the travel accessory business are still doing fine, selling leather upholstery or audio systems or whatever.

"The second rule is *learn to dance*. That means dancing with everyone you work with: all your customers, all your distributors, all your suppliers, everyone. I like that — the more we learn to dance with people, smoothly and skillfully, and give them what they want with the best possible service and quality of product, the easier it is to achieve our goals. Our working relationships should be a dance, not a struggle. With ease and lightness, not stress and strain. Creatively working with people so that everyone's happy. Finding win-win solutions — dancing together! It's a wonderful way to put it."

I realized Bernie did everything with ease and lightness. It was a kind of dance working with him — more like a game that he played with great enjoyment. And it occurred to me that real mastery — whether in playing an instrument or running a business — means doing something with ease and grace. Bernie had certainly created *success with ease* — and that's a wonderful goal for all of us.

"Do you remember the third rule?"

"Something about J. Edgar Hoover..." was all I could remember.

"*Leave J. Edgar Hoover behind*. Do you know what that means?"

"Not really — something to do with avoiding secrecy, or paranoia?"

"J. Edgar Hoover was famous — *infamous*, rather — for his endless control of his employees' actions. His management style was completely dictatorial. Everything came from the top down; management told everyone exactly what to do. At least, that was the reputation he had.

"Leaving him behind means giving employees responsibility to do their job in their own way. It's the kind of 'hands-off' management policy that Hoover would hate. Hire good people, clearly define their responsibility, and let them do it their own way. They're the ones in the trenches, after all, doing their jobs all day. Get responsible people, and let them do their jobs as they see fit. As I've said many times before, treat employees like adults, and they'll act like adults. Treat them like children, and they'll act like children."

He took a long, thoughtful sip of his coffee before he continued.

"Instead of management from the top down, it should be management from the bottom up. There has to be someone on top, one person responsible for the success of the whole operation, responsible for the vision, the long-range view of the company, and for the business plan that translates the long-range view into the next short-term steps to take. But the people doing the work should be completely responsible for managing their jobs. They should tell the president how they can best do their jobs, not the other way around.

"I've heard so many employers moan about how hard it is to find good people — I tell you, that says much more about those employers than it does about people in general. I've never had problems finding good people, never. Or keeping them. The world is full of good people, if they're treated with respect, treated as adults. If you assume they're responsible, they act responsibly. If you challenge them, they rise to the challenge. There are exceptions, of course, but the vast majority of people I've hired have done really well in their work.

"There's just one simple rule I use in hiring people: Hire people who are *passionate* about that job. There are many different kinds of people in the world, and many different kinds of jobs. Some jobs are repetitive and require a lot of detail work and organization. There are a lot of people who love doing that kind of work — and other people who are driven nuts by that kind of work.

"A very perceptive woman I know named Nancy Anderson wrote a book called *Work with Passion*, and in it she says there are three kinds of people — technicians, managers, and entrepreneurs. The technicians like to do the detail work. They like hands-on, nitty-gritty tasks. They like the sense of accomplishment a completed project gives them. All too often they do so well they're promoted to management positions, and a lot of them just aren't suited to management. They don't necessarily like to deal with a lot of people; they'd rather be doing the work itself.

"A good manager works well with people. They enjoy sitting down with a group of people and solving problems or brainstorming. They work well in teams.

"The entrepreneurs, on the other hand, have the most

fun when they're taking risks, starting up new things, new projects.

"They're three very different types of energy — and you need them all, in every organization of any size.

"Now, a whole lot of people do two or three of those things. I do them all, at times — I love certain kinds of detail work, I work in management, and I love to start new things, too. I'll bet you do them all, too. But you're probably happier doing one of those things than the others.

"*Real success* is doing what you love to do, all the time, isn't it? At least that's what I call success. Having the time and freedom and resources to do what you love, all the time. To work when you feel like it. Goof off when you feel like it. Enjoy what you're doing, every day — that's success.

"Here's a good test: If you want to see whether a person is a manager or an entrepreneur, look at their garage — a manager's garage is neat as a pin, with outlines on the wall showing where to hang each tool, and an entrepreneur's garage is a mess, filled with half-completed or barely begun projects."

I had to laugh at that; according to that test, I was certainly an entrepreneur, not a manager.

"It's an overgeneralization, but it makes a good point: You've got to hire a technician for a technician's job, a manager for a manager's job. And don't hire entrepreneurs at all, because they won't be happy working for you, unless you have some real creative project they can develop, ideally something where they can eventually get equity — at least some percentage of ownership."

He stared at his ham sandwich.

"They must have a new chef. This sandwich is different than it was last week. Hmm . . ."

He examined the sandwich, slowly, taking the bread off the top and looking inside.

"You know, this shows another important principle: *Be consistent.* In a changing world, people want as much consistency as possible. McDonald's is a lousy hamburger, but it's absolutely the same lousy hamburger all over the country — probably all over the world, I don't know. I've never eaten at a McDonald's in Russia or China. But anywhere you go in the U.S., it's absolutely the same hamburger. It's exactly what everyone has come to expect. Look at the huge mistake Coca-Cola made when they tampered with their formula. They finally recovered, with their 'Classic Coke,' but they made a huge, expensive blunder because they forgot the principle of *consistency.*

"Try to be as consistent as possible with everyone you deal with. Try to create the best products you possibly can, and give the best service possible — and then be as consistent as you possibly can. That's a challenge for you."

I had to agree.

SUMMARY

- *Love change* — or at least learn to accept it. The world is changing all the time. Those who have the vision to use change to their advantage survive and prosper.

- *Learn to dance.* Your working relationships should be a dance, not a struggle. Learn to dance with people, smoothly and skillfully, with ease and lightness. Create a win-win situation; give them what they want with the best possible service and quality, and you'll reach your goals.

- *Leave J. Edgar Hoover behind.* Top-down, dictatorial management that tells everyone exactly what to do is inefficient, is prone to serious mistakes, and undermines employee morale. Hire competent people, clearly define their responsibilities, and let them do it their own way. Treat them like responsible adults, and they'll act like responsible adults.

- Hire people who are passionate about their jobs and who have the suitable personality for the job: Hire a technician for a technician's job and a manager for a manager's job.

- In a changing world, people want as much consistency as possible. Try to create the best products you possibly can and give the best service possible — then be as consistent as you possibly can. This is a key to success.

KEY NINE

*Reflect on the events that have shaped your life
and discover the core beliefs you have created
for yourself because of those events.*

THINGS WERE STARTING TO MOVE FORWARD, though it was still a bumpy ride. We hadn't achieved our goals, but we were at least beginning to make some progress. The stodgy barge I had pictured the business to be was beginning to move a little bit, at least in my imagination, but it was still encountering a lot of choppy waves and wind and other kinds of resistance.

A month or so passed, very quickly, before I heard from Bernie again. He called and invited me out to his home for lunch. I jumped at the chance — I was curious to see what his home looked like. He lived outside of the city, in a beautiful hilly area. I drove out there on a Friday afternoon, a lovely autumn day. The air was clear; it had that special rich smell of autumn woods.

As I drove out there, I told myself I had to get out of the office more often. I had to get away from the business, occasionally, to get a fresh perspective on things.

The directions to Bernie's were a bit complex; he lived quite a way off the main road. After roaming around a bit, I found his gate, which was open. His long driveway climbed up a wooded hill and finally circled around in front of his home, a beautiful white one-story structure nestled in the pines.

Bernie greeted me at the door wearing a sweat suit and moccasins. His hair was immaculately combed, as usual. He managed to look pretty sharp. We rambled through his home; he gave me a complete tour, stopping to explain where a particular piece of art or furniture came from.

Different rooms had different themes: The living room had a look of the Southwest desert; it was filled with native art from North and South America, and with his wife's original paintings. His family room, off the dining room, was filled with Asian art: screens with exotic floral designs, paintings on cloth from Tibet and India. And, to my surprise, there was a room for meditation and yoga, furnished sparingly, mainly with cushions, a sound system, and a sitting Buddha that radiated a quiet, peaceful energy.

Behind the house was a swimming pool with a hot tub on one end. The house and pool were on the top of a hill, and the view was inspiring. There was a building off to the left, and another to the right, perfectly symmetrical. The one on the left was a guesthouse, furnished in an Americana theme — it looked like a farmhouse from a century ago, complete with a hand pump on the edge of the kitchen sink. The building on the right was a large, airy artist's studio, with windows all around showing off the view.

Bernie's wife was inside the studio. Her name was Lucia, and it fit her well: She was radiant, filled with light and laughter. She was working on a painting that shimmered color, reminiscent of South America, where she was from originally. Her thick hair was held back from her face with a colorful cloth — no, it was more than a cloth, it had sparkling jewels in it.

She seemed glad to meet me, and I felt happy for Bernie that he had found such a woman to be his wife — and happy for her that she had found such a man. There was a warm, obvious affection between the two.

Lucia kept painting, and Bernie and I went back to the kitchen, where he had a big lazy Susan on the table with two platters on it, one filled with meats and cheeses and avocado slices and crackers, and the other piled full of grapes, tangerines, papayas, and mangoes. He brewed up a delicious cup of coffee as well.

After we feasted, we moved into the living room with the coffee and sat in front of a picture window with a view of endless rolling pine-covered hills that became more and more luminescent in the distance. It was a view that took your breath away, a view that looked like a romantic painting. I was sure the house had been built primarily to feature that spectacular view.

We sat in silence in front of the window. Our lunch had been a late and leisurely one, and the sun was already getting low in the west.

"I sit here for hours, just staring out this window," said Bernie. "It's a good way to meditate."

Several minutes passed in silence, and I saw exactly what Bernie meant. I felt peaceful, happy just to be sitting there, comfortably in silence, watching the light play in the clouds and on the tree-covered hills.

Bernie finally broke the silence. He spoke quietly.

"It's good to meditate, in some form, whether it's sitting or walking or camping or lying flat on your back, or whatever. Whatever you can do to be quiet for a while, away from the radio and TV. There are all kinds of benefits of meditation — countless physical, mental, emotional, and spiritual benefits.

"One of the best things about meditation is that it tunes you in to that still, small voice within, the voice of your intuition. We all have many inner voices, and the way to identify the voice of our intuition is that it's calm and clear and self-assured, always — and it feels positive and supportive, always. Our intuition always knows what is perfectly right for us, in the moment. Look within, and you'll find every answer you need."

He quietly stressed that last sentence.

"To be successful in life, you've got to be intuitive — you've got to learn to discover your intuition and to trust it. You don't need to meditate, necessarily, to find it; it's just gut instinct. It's just following your internal guidance system. We all have one.

"I bet on you because my intuition tells me you're following your intuition. And that's all you need, ultimately, to be successful. Your intuition will guide you into doing the right thing at the right moment, and doing what you're here on earth to do.

"You don't need an MBA, or accounting courses, or consultants. You don't need to copy other successful businesses. Just do what is in your heart to do — and you will be led, step by step, to reach your goals. The next step to take will always be clear to you, and then the next — it'll be obvious."

Several more minutes passed in silence. It was quiet as a temple in his living room. I didn't remember ever being in a place of total silence; it made me aware of my thoughts, which were going constantly, like a radio. It made me aware of how little meditation I had done. I felt honored to be able to sit in the peaceful stillness Bernie and Lucia had created in their home.

HE FINALLY SPOKE AGAIN, quietly: "I've been thinking about something today, something that affects us so much, and yet is rarely talked about. I've been thinking about the powerful people and events that shape our lives, and how important it is to reflect on them, occasionally, and see the deep, underlying beliefs we have created for ourselves because of those people and those events."

I glanced from the window and looked at Bernie. He was sitting comfortably back in his chair, his hands forming a little temple in front of his chest, almost as if he were in prayer.

"Every company reflects the consciousness of the president or CEO. That's a fact. Yet it's so rare that business owners — or anyone else — understand the importance of examining their lives, and examining how their minds operate, in order to create a better life, and a more successful business as well.

"So many people sabotage themselves, needlessly, because of unexamined core beliefs about how the world operates. I had a mentor, many years ago. He was brilliant, and taught me a lot. Yet he also had some horribly negative core beliefs that affected his life and his business.

"He believed you had to struggle to create a successful business — and so, of course, his business was an endless struggle. He believed you had to work hard, so hard that it was bad for your health — and so, of course, he was in poor health, all through his later years. And he believed there wasn't enough time to accomplish everything that needed to be done, so he never took the time to enjoy life, to take vacations, to get to know his family, to develop other interests.

"Here's the strange thing about our beliefs — I think it's strange, anyway. I think it's downright weird, but the beliefs we have are not true in themselves — many, many people obviously have very different sets of beliefs than we do. But our beliefs become self-fulfilling if we believe them! *All our core beliefs are self-fulfilling.*

"It's impossible to create a successful business without believing — deeply — that you're capable of building a successful business. It's impossible to live abundantly without believing that you deserve abundance, and that you can manage money wisely.

"My mentor was like a lot of successful people: He believed he knew how to create a successful business, but he also believed a lot of garbage that really hurt the quality of his life. I wish I knew then what I know now — I would have told him what I'm telling you. Not that he would have listened, of course. His beliefs were too deeply ingrained; he wasn't open to change. He wouldn't even have dared to examine his beliefs and see how they affected his life. And the unexamined life is not worth living."

I had heard that before, but the way Bernie phrased it gave it new meaning.

"Socrates said that. I don't think he meant it as a judgment call, to say that people who don't examine their lives lead worthless lives. I think he meant that, if you don't examine your life, the kind of life you create is so far inferior to what you could have that it's probably better off not to have lived that life at all. We're here to grow, to learn, to build a better and better life for ourselves and others — and if we don't fulfill that promise, we'll always feel unfulfilled."

There was another moment of silence.

"It's very important — in some cases *critical* — to take some time to examine our lives. The first thing to do is to look at our past — as honestly as we can — and remember those people and events and influences that have shaped our lives.

"We've all had many things in our lives that have shaped the way we move and talk, the way we think, the way we perceive the world. The events and people that have given rise to our core beliefs about the world, about ourselves, about the nature of reality.

"Some people have had a great many painful events like abuse or other kinds of violence. Some shaping events are the results of painful experiences, some are the results of powerfully positive experiences, some are the results of the simplest moment, the simplest word from someone at the right time — or the wrong time — that we have carried with us ever since.

"Some of these shaping events have led to very good core beliefs — and those moments should be remembered, and those beliefs encouraged and supported. Almost all of us have had someone in our lives who saw our potential and supported us in some way. Even kids in the worst circumstances usually have someone who inspires them in some way — a teacher or parent or relative or *someone.* Or else they find a wellspring of inspiration somewhere in themselves.

"Here's something I'm convinced of: Every one of us is a creative genius, in some unique way. Every one of us was born with some gift to give the world. Many of us have trouble seeing what it is, because it's so natural to us. But, deep down, we know it intuitively: We have a great gift to share with other people.

"We've all had glimpses of our genius, at some time in our lives, and we've all had other forces that have sought to crush our genius, through doubt, through cynicism, through all kinds of limiting or negative beliefs.

"We need to reflect on these things every once in a while. Those shaping moments that have had a negative impact on us need to be looked at, and we need to see the negative — or *limiting* — core beliefs we formed as a result.

"Once those beliefs are identified, and clearly expressed, they can be let go of. Because they're not true — they're simply self-fulfilling things that become true if we believe them. This is the process of becoming *conscious* — becoming aware of the forces that drive us, and learning how to act on those forces. When we do that, we learn how to shape our destiny, how to become powerful and achieve what we want in life.

"That's why it's so valuable to write an autobiography — I think everyone should write their autobiography. Or at least reflect on the moments that forged our core beliefs, at least describe and remember the shaping moments in our lives.

"Every one of us is a creative genius. And every child knows it! But then we grow up, and we gather a collection of garbage beliefs that trash our belief in ourselves. It's important to examine those beliefs, and dump that garbage.

"I think it was Emerson who said that we wouldn't have been given our desires in the first place if we didn't have the capability of fulfilling them. You are capable of anything — anything your heart desires. There are no limits to what you can accomplish — *if you believe it to be true*. What you believe to be true becomes true, in your experience. So examine your beliefs, and focus on and remember only those beliefs that empower you."

Bernie spoke with a quiet authority. His words were inspiring, and I hoped I could remember them.

"Believe in yourself enough to believe this: If you focus on your goal, on your dream, often enough, it will become an *intention*. You have the capability, within you, to turn your most important desires into intentions — and your intentions will manifest in reality. It's a law of nature. *Intentions produce results.*

"Our thoughts and our words are powerful — powerful enough to create what we want in life."

There was silence once again. The sky was a fragile eggshell blue painted with chimerical wisps of delicate pink clouds. The sun was beginning to set, in an awe-inspiring display of what is possible.

"So be it. So it is," he whispered.

SUMMARY

- It's good to get away from your business occasionally to gain a fresh perspective on your work and your life.
- It's good to meditate in some form, whether it's sitting or walking or camping or lying flat on your back or whatever. There are all kinds of benefits of meditation: physical, mental, emotional, and spiritual.
- Through meditation, you discover the calm and clear and self-assured voice of your intuition. There are other ways to find it — you don't *need* to meditate — but to be successful in your career and fulfilled in your life, you've got to be intuitive — to trust and act on your intuition.
- Every business reflects the consciousness of the top person: the president or CEO. Yet so few business leaders understand the importance of examining their lives, and examining how their minds operate, in order for them to create a better life and a more successful business.
- We all have deep core beliefs created during childhood and young adulthood, and though they are not true in themselves, they become self-fulfilling in our lives if we believe them. Our positive core beliefs — such as the belief that we are capable and creative and intuitive — should be supported and encouraged. Our negative or limiting core beliefs — such

as the belief that it is hard to succeed, and highly stressful, and can only be done at great personal sacrifice — should be identified and let go of. Remember: Our negative core beliefs are not true — they are simply self-fulfilling; they become true if we believe them.

- Every one of us is a creative genius, in some way. There are no limits to what you can accomplish — if you believe it to be true. When you focus long enough on your goals and dreams, they become *intentions* — and your intentions will eventually manifest in reality. It is a law of nature: *Intentions produce results.*

KEY TEN

Evolve through the three stages of a business:
infancy, adolescence, adulthood.

I was growing to enjoy my time with Bernie immensely. I took notes after each of our encounters; my pile of notes was growing into a little book. I'd often page through the notes, and I'd always find something inspiring or useful — usually both — for the challenges and opportunities I was facing at that moment.

Bernie called a few weeks after I had been to his house, and he asked me to meet him in a state park area that was not too far from the city. I was only too happy to get out of the office — it had been a difficult week. I needed a break. And I looked forward to seeing Bernie again.

We met in the parking lot. Bernie was there when I arrived, dressed in a sweat suit and well-worn running shoes, sitting comfortably on the hood of his car, with his feet on the bumper. He looked like a large gargoyle hood ornament.

We walked through the woods, briskly at times, enough to work up a sweat. The trees were swaying in the wind, shimmering with the brilliance of autumn.

He asked how the business was going. I told him we hadn't reached our projections — in fact we were short by quite a bit. I was disappointed, I had to admit — we'd been doing better when I last reported to him, and now we were slipping rather than moving ahead.

"What are you planning on doing in sales for the year?" Bernie asked.

This time I had the answer for him immediately. It had become emblazoned in my mind. Bernie chuckled appreciatively.

"Don't worry if you're short of your goals at first," he said. "It almost always happens that way. The growth of a business is an organic thing; it takes time. It's taken many years for all these strong, solid trees to grow — and it'll take years for you to grow a strong, solid business."

He wandered off the path and over to a magnificent pine that towered over us. "Look at this tree," he said. He raised both hands and put them on the tree, communing silently with it for a moment. "Our lives are like this tree — and your business is like this tree: It will grow and grow, until it casts its seeds to the wind...and many of those seeds will grow, and many of them won't.

"Some years, the trees get a lot of rain, and there's an explosion of growth. Some years, when it's dry, they barely grow at all. Sometimes there are years of drought, and they retrench, and don't grow one bit.

"It's the same with your business. . . ." The sentence wandered off a bit, and Bernie went wandering off as well, into the trees.

"EVERY BUSINESS GOES THROUGH THREE STAGES," Bernie said, after we had trekked along for a while in silence.

"Infancy, adolescence, and adulthood. You're still in your infancy, so you have to be patient, just like you have to be patient with a baby. A business in its infancy has to be constantly fed and nurtured, watched and guarded. It's still vulnerable, and it has a big appetite. You have to keep giving to it, and you can't expect anything in return.

"But as long as you're patient and you stick to your plan and keep your goals clearly in mind, one day you'll find your baby has become an adolescent. Now it can support itself, but no one else. It's important at this stage that you don't try to treat it like a mature business. It's still young. Don't draw too much out of the business. Be very careful about expanding too quickly. Growth should be slow and steady, like these trees, or like an adolescent boy or girl.

"Finally, if you keep your goals clear in your mind, and keep moving ahead in any way you can, your business will reach its goals and become a true adult. It'll be mature, powerful, able to support you and many others abundantly.

"When you reach that point, I want you to do a few things: First of all, take a vacation. A long, well-deserved period of rest and relaxation. Then take regular vacations after that. You've got to get away from the business every once in a while, and relax, and get a clearer perspective on your business and your life.

"When your business has reached adulthood, it can pay everyone a good salary as well as a substantial share of the profits. Keep salaries reasonable — competitive with industry standards, but on the generous side — and reward yourself and everyone else with profit sharing.

"When your business has reached this point, here's something else I recommend: Send your parents a big bonus check, if they're still alive. Send it to them whether they need it or not.

"It's something I did as soon as my first company started making money. I just did it on a whim, because I kept fantasizing about doing it. But after I did it, I realized it was one of the single best things I ever did. It totally surprised and delighted my parents, of course. But it was an even better experience for me. By making that gesture, I told myself, as well as my parents, that I was an adult now and could support myself — and even support them if need be. It sent a powerful message to my subconscious mind that I was ready, willing, and able to create a mature, powerful company, one that could support me and a lot of others abundantly. It's far more than just a gift; it's a confirmation of your expanding power."

We reached a pond nestled in the trees. Bernie picked up a stone and skipped it expertly across the water. It carved a long arc across the still surface, skipping ten or twelve times before it finally sank.

"Nice job, Bernie."

"I've had lots of practice."

I picked up a flat, round stone and gave it my best shot. It skipped once, then sank abruptly.

"Hmm, I guess I need more practice," I said. It had been more years than I cared to remember since I had skipped stones into a pond.

We spent the next twenty minutes or so playing like children. I finally found the perfect stone that skipped in a long arc, like Bernie's first one had done. I was surprised at how good it felt, even though my arm ached. For a moment there, I was as elated as a six-year-old.

We strolled on, and Bernie picked up right where he had left off.

"Once your business is in its adulthood, use your money wisely. Always keep some in reserve, so the company has the strength to weather difficult times — and there probably will be difficult times; there are for nearly all businesses. The economy is cyclical. The companies that have cash reserves can weather all the cycles.

"You should have some personal cash reserves, too, that you can draw on and even loan back to the company if necessary. Don't get overextended with big mortgage payments, a vacation home, and other things that have a constant monthly payment. Live frugally for a while, pay off your credit card debt, and get ahead of the game with some substantial savings. Then you can go out and buy that vacation home, or boat, or whatever you want.

"And once the company starts making profits, give away

at least 5 to 10 percent of your profits: Donate to worthy organizations — there are thousands of them that are worth supporting."

I was a little unclear on his concept. "How does this fit in with what you said earlier, when you said to retain what the business needed, and then split the rest between the owners and employees?"

Bernie explained carefully: "First you have your total pretax profit — the bottom line of the company's annual profit and loss statement, right?"

"Right."

"Then you need to retain in the company as much as you and your banker and your CPA or financial advisers — whoever you consult — feel the company needs. This is the amount you pay taxes on. So first you subtract your retained earnings. Then take 5 to 10 percent of the remaining amount and donate it to the nonprofits of your choice. Then split the rest fifty-fifty between the owners and the employees. At least, that's what I recommend. You may find a different formula that works better for you.

"Tithing 5 or 10 percent is not only generous, it's good business. It's great public relations for the company. But it's far more than that as well: To be really successful with money, you've got to give it away. There's something mystical about the tithing principle — it expands you, so that more money comes to you.

"Personally, give at least 10 percent away, too, so you're contributing on both fronts: business and personal. Don't use the excuse, 'I gave at the office.' Give at home *and* at the office. And a magical thing will happen: You'll never want for money. You'll be surrounded by abundance. The universe will keep showering you with riches.

"Give to charities, give to friends, relatives, people on the street; give to environmental groups and human rights groups and children's organizations; give to your church if you go to church; give to the local soup kitchen, the local shelter, the abused women's shelter, homes for children, schools, youth programs; give to anything and anyone that moves you to give. Just make sure it's at least 10 percent of your income. You'll never regret it.

"Once your business is successful, one of the greatest, most satisfying things you can do is to support all kinds of worthwhile things, and people. We've been doing a good thing at my companies for years: Take that 5 or 10 percent of the profits and divide it up equally among all the employees. Then you ask them what organizations they want to support, and you donate it along with a note saying this donation is from that employee.

"At first, when I set it up, I had no idea of the amount of goodwill it would create, both in the company and in the world!

"I support a lot of good causes. I'm doing my bit for the earth and for humanity: Greenpeace, Children International, Amnesty International, Sierra Club, World Wildlife Fund, the Nature Conservancy, the local homeless shelter, the abused women's shelter, Brazil Hope — the group my wife is involved with. The list goes on and on. And I invest in all kinds of things as well, and I love it. It's just as gratifying for me as it is for the people I invest in.

"I'm investing in you, for example, and helping in my way to make your dream a reality. And I'm enjoying it as much or maybe even more than you are.

"The more you give, the more you receive — and not just financially, though it's true financially. But you receive far more important things as well — satisfaction, contentment, fulfillment. And even love.

"And that's the most important thing of all."

SUMMARY

- The growth of a business is an organic thing, just like the growth of a large, strong tree — both take years to develop. Both have years when growth is explosive; both have years when there is little or no growth. Be as patient with your business as you would be with a pine or oak seedling.

- Every business goes through three stages: infancy, adolescence, and adulthood. A business in its infancy has to be constantly fed and nurtured, watched and guarded. You have to keep giving to it, and you can't expect anything in return.

- Once a business has reached adolescence, it can support itself, but no one else. It's important at this stage that you don't try to treat it like a mature business. It's still young. Don't draw too much out of the business. Be very careful about expanding too quickly. Growth should be slow and steady.

- If you keep your goals clearly in mind, your business will reach those goals eventually and become a true adult. It will be mature and powerful, able to support you and many others abundantly.

- Once your business is in its adulthood, use your money wisely. Always keep some in reserve, so the business has the strength to weather difficult times — and there probably will be difficult times; there are for nearly all businesses. The economy is cyclical.

The companies that have cash reserves can weather all the cycles.

- You should have personal cash reserves as well that you can draw on and even loan back to the company if necessary. Don't get too overextended with big monthly payments; pay off your credit card debt and get ahead of the game with some substantial savings.

- Once the company starts making profits, give away 5 to 10 percent of your profits to worthy nonprofit organizations. Divide the amount you're contributing by the number of your employees, and give that amount in each employee's name to the organizations he or she wants to support. This generates a huge amount of goodwill in the company, your community, and the world.

- The more you give, the more you receive — and not just financially. You receive far more important things as well: satisfaction, contentment, fulfillment, and love.

KEY ELEVEN

Consider the spiritual and mystical
side of business:
Practice your own form of effective magic.

I WAS STILL STRUGGLING with a company in its infant stage with a somewhat clueless staff (including myself), and I was an exasperated and impatient parent at times. When I look back on it, there were deeper reasons for my frustration than purely financial ones. On a deep level — on what Bernie would describe as a *core belief* level — I had my doubts and fears about everything I was doing. I doubted myself. I even doubted the worthiness of building a business in the first place. Some part of me believed that if I succeeded in business, I would lose my soul in some way. I'd become consumed by materialism, and forget my creativity, my friends and family, and my higher purpose in it all.

I had insistent doubts about my ability to do what

needed to be done, and insistent fears about the direction my life would take if it turned out I was somehow able to build a successful business. Perhaps Bernie was aware of my thoughts; perhaps he had gone through a similar stage when he was young. I wanted to ask him, but when I was with him, the question just never came up.

In light of all this, our next meeting was remarkable.

SEVERAL WEEKS PASSED before I heard from Bernie again. Then he called on a Friday afternoon and said, "Look, there's a full moon on Monday. Why don't you come out to my place in time for the sunset and moonrise?"

We watched the sunset from his living room and then went out by his pool to watch an almost unbelievably large, brilliant orange harvest moon rise slowly over the shadowy trees. The lights were on in Lucia's studio; she was apparently painting.

"On nights like this, I love to sit in the hot tub," Bernie said. "Want to join me?"

It seemed like a good idea. The night was cool; the tub was hot. We had to get in slowly. Bernie's body was lean and supple. It was quite a surprise to see him in such good shape.

"Ahh . . ." Bernie said. He took several seconds to say the word. He exhaled deeply, several times, and faced the rising moon. He looked much younger than his years. His eyes were large and clear.

"This kind of night, this full moon, is very special," he said. He spoke quietly but intensely.

"I've given you everything you need to understand the

mechanics of successful business. How it works. It's not all that complicated; anyone can do it. *Anyone.* Even you. Don't worry.

"If you can remember even just a little bit of what I've said, and apply it, you'll be successful. Because all it involves is remembering to stop and take a long-term view of things occasionally. Look at the big picture every once in a while. Make sure that picture includes moving steadily toward your dreams."

He was quiet for a long moment.

"We live in an exciting time. It used to be that science and religion were polar opposites. They seemed to have two completely different methods: religion and metaphysics were intuitive, based on faith; science was rational. God! They were even violently opposed to each other over and over throughout history.

"But in the twentieth century, science and metaphysics merged. Physicists discovered what the metaphysical types had believed for centuries: It is only our crude sense of sight that makes it appear as if we are totally different individuals — as Einstein put it, our separateness is an 'optical illusion.' We are in reality all one, in one quantum field, eternally interconnected in one vast ocean of atoms. And those atoms are composed of empty space, yet filled with whirling forces of energy and information. Buddhists have been chanting for thousands of years: *'Form is emptiness; emptiness is form.'* Physicists have discovered this is true."

When he said, *Form is emptiness, emptiness is form,* he chanted the words.

"Some people call it the New Age!" He chuckled. "It's a fine term, but there's nothing new in the new age. The Bhagavad Gita was written over five thousand years ago! It's straight from the source, and the source of so many other teachings.

"These teachings have been available throughout history, and reinvented every generation — though we haven't done a very good job of practicing the teachings of the Gita, and Jesus, and Buddha, and Muhammad, and all the other great teachers and prophets.

"James Allen wrote *As You Think* in 1904. It's all in that book. Everything. Israel Regardie wrote *The Art of True Healing* in the 1930s. It's filled with powerful creative meditations; it's Western magic in a nutshell. The so-called New Age philosophy is the Perennial Philosophy that Aldous Huxley described — it's as old as humankind.

"For myself, I've boiled its essence down to something that's very simple. That's the way it has to be, for me — simple and clear — to have an impact on my life."

He sat in silence for a moment, gazing at the moon, before he continued.

"There are many paths up the mountain. And every one of us is absolutely unique and finds what we need to find in our own way, on our own terms, and in our own words. We each make our own absolutely unique contribution to the vast, ever-growing archives of the Perennial Philosophy — or the New Age or spiritual quest or higher consciousness or the human potential movement or the 12-step programs or whatever else you want to call it.

"My parents were Jewish. But I didn't see, didn't really understand, the wisdom in my own tradition when I was young. I studied the vast wisdom traditions of India as a young man, and I found guidance and answers.

"I learned about *dharma* — the teachings, the laws of the universe, and the importance for each of us to discover our higher purpose in life, our mission, and to fulfill that purpose.

"I learned about *karma* — all of us are rewarded with the fruits of our thoughts and actions, whether they're good or bad. The good person encounters goodness and success; the misguided person who doesn't understand karma encounters pain and failure. Each of us creates our own experience of the world; we have no one else to blame for our failures. At some point, we realize that *every moment* of our lives has been absolutely perfect. Every moment has its use, its teaching for us.

"I went to India when I was young...." He smiled at the memory. "I met a teacher who told me my mind was way too active. He tied a string to my wrist and tied the other end to a turtle, and told me to stay with that turtle for three days. And I did it. I have never been the same since." He laughed heartily.

"I learned about meditation in India: the importance of learning to quiet the mind. Once our mind begins to quiet, our intuitive mind starts speaking to us, in a still, small voice. Actually, it's been speaking to us all the time, but we just never heard it, because it was drowned out by the constant chatter in our heads. Meditation shows us how to *listen within*.

"I learned to do yoga. That's why I'm in such good shape. That and my fruit juice — I drink lots of fruit juice, morning and evening. And I do a bit of yoga nearly every day, even if it's just a Sun Salutation or two.

"My yoga teacher told me to close my eyes when doing yoga, and 'see God.' She said it so simply, so plainly, and I've never forgotten it.

"Then I came back to this country and looked to the Christian tradition, and found answers and guidance there, too, of course. Christ taught about karma when he said, 'As you sow, so shall you reap.' And St. Paul had taught about moderation — 'the Golden Mean' — just as Buddha had taught about taking the middle road, the path between all extremes, the path of moderation in everything.

"I read the Bible. The words of Christ are still brilliant today. It's sad to me that so many people proclaiming to be Christian somehow manage to ignore so many of the words of Christ. How can you call yourself a Christian and still want to carry firearms or build atom bombs or enforce the death penalty? What would Christ's reaction be to those people? 'Peter, put away your sword — if you live by the sword, by the sword you die.' You can't say it much clearer than that.

"So many institutions have risen, churches and governments, that proclaim to be Christian, but have forgotten the words of their founder!"

He quoted easily from memory:

"Love your enemies, bless them that curse you, do good

to them that hate you, and pray for those who spitefully use you, and persecute you.... Turn the other cheek....

"Judge not, lest you be judged.... He that is without sin among you, let him cast the first stone....

"A new law I give unto you: Love one another, as I have loved you.

"Ask and you shall receive, seek and you will find, knock and the door will be opened unto you.... The Kingdom of Heaven is within."

We both gazed at the silent full moon for a while. Then Bernie went on.

"I looked at the traditions of indigenous peoples all over the world as well, and found guidance and answers. They all believe in the sacredness of life, the sacredness of the earth. Our earth is our Mother — she has literally provided us the materials for our bodies — so we need to respect and cherish her.

"They all believe in worlds beyond this world of ours. 'There is no death,' Chief Joseph said, 'Only a change of worlds.'

"They believe the dead have power, and need to be honored and respected. We need to live in a way that our ancestors would be proud of, because the spirits of our ancestors are still with us, still part of us. Just as Christians believe you can feel the spirit of Christ living in your heart, so indigenous people feel the spirits of their ancestors, living and breathing through them.

"I've studied Western mysticism, too, and found answers

and inspiration. I learned that real magic exists. I learned simple magical rituals for health, problem solving, prosperity, love. . . . As long as you understand karma, magic is a powerful tool that can work for you.

"And that led me right back to Judaism, because much of Western magic is based on it. And I finally found answers and inspiration within my own roots, right back where I started.

"One of the best ways to express all these various teachings in the simplest and clearest way — and this may or may not surprise you — is from the 12-step programs, originally from Alcoholics Anonymous. God help and bless all the alcoholics out there! The twelve steps are brilliant.

"The third step says, *I made a decision to turn my will and my life over to the care of God, as I understand God.* That leads right to the eleventh step, *I sought through prayer and meditation to improve my conscious contact with God as I understand God, praying only for knowledge of God's will and the power to carry it out.*

"That's it, in a nutshell — at least for me: *Just keep turning it over to God, asking to do God's will.* That's a simple solution. Whenever you have a problem, turn it over to God — whatever you believe God or a higher power or the creative force of the universe to be.

"Whenever you have a question, ask it, and then listen within for the answer. *Ask, and you shall receive.*"

THERE WAS A QUIET PAUSE, as we gazed at the moon in silence. The water was warm and satisfying. I felt no need to say anything. Bernie finally broke the silence.

"So, one of the most important things we can do is reflect on what we believe God to be. What is God in our lives? What do we really believe? What makes sense for us? What is reasonable, for each of us, given our unique background and culture and beliefs? It's good to think about this, and come up with *something* — because that conception of God can provide us with all the answers and guidance and inspiration we need to create the life we dream of creating.

"Everyone has some conception of a higher power — even if they call themselves atheists they still have some idea of, some name for, the forces that created this universe. As I've said to many people many times before, if you don't believe in a higher power, go make a blade of grass. Or a cricket. Or a galaxy. Some power created those things — how do you describe that power? Chemistry? Then that's your higher power. Atomic energy? Then that's your description of what I choose to call God, the forces of creation, of life. Call it what you will; it doesn't matter to me. You can just call it the Universe. You can call it the Force. You can call it *life*.

"In the Native American traditions, God is called the Great Mystery. We'll never understand God; God is the force of creation, eternally mysterious. God is the force within the atoms, the intelligence that forms the complex structures of all matter. God is the force within the galaxies, the force that causes stars to be born and to spawn life and to spectacularly die. God is the force that causes the simple elements that have been blasted out from those dying stars to combine and form all living things, including molecules as complex as the DNA in every cell of our body. We'll never really understand those forces, in their essence. It's the Great Mystery of our existence.

"Every one of us, each in our own way, experiences that Great Mystery. It is the mystery of our birth, of every moment of our lives, and of our death. . . .

"DO YOU BELIEVE IN GOD?" He didn't give me time to answer the question.

"To me, that question is exactly the same as, *Do you believe in the creative power of the Universe?* Or, *Do you believe a tiny seed can grow to a huge tree?* Or, *Do you believe in physics?*

"The answer to all these questions is obvious to me — and has nothing to do with belief.

"Whenever you have a problem — of any kind at all — turn it over to the forces of creation, to God as you understand God. You can call this process prayer, or you can call it anything you like. Just say, 'Well, Creator (or whatever you want to call it, or him, or her), I put the problem in your hands — I'm turning it over to you. Just show me what your will is. Let me do your will.'

"Turn everything over to God, and let God work out the details.

"Just keep asking to do God's will, and your problems will dissolve. You will be shown, step by step, intuitively, what to do.

"You never need to worry about your business once you turn it over to God. For you aren't in charge of your business anymore — God is the new president. And chairman of the board as well.

"Just keep asking what God's will is, and you'll be guided to do exactly the right thing for you. You might take the company in completely unexpected directions! It doesn't matter — God is showing you where and how to go. God is directing the show.

"I talk to God every morning. I wander out here, and thank the creative power behind all this for everything there is, and everything we've been given. Every day, I find something new to be thankful for. My gratitude list is endless.

"And then I say, 'Guide me'... and I listen. And God says nearly the same thing to me, every morning: *'Love, serve, and remember.'*

"Remember what? *'Remember to love and serve, always. Love and serve yourself and others.'*

"Over the years I've seen how practical and powerful those words are: *love and serve.* Let those words guide you in your business and your life, always. Love and serve yourself, and your employees, and your customers — everyone you come into contact with.

"That's the greatest business advice of all. It will guide you to do the right thing, always."

I'd been completely absorbed in his words, trying to remember as many as possible. I suddenly became aware that I was extremely hot; my hair was soaked with sweat. Bernie read my mind, or the beet-red color of my face.

"Let's get out of here," he said.

HE PLUNGED INTO THE POOL, and I followed. It was cold;
it was exhilarating.

We toweled off and dressed again and went inside the
house. Bernie opened the door of his refrigerator; I saw an
entire shelf filled with different kinds of fruit juices. We
both got a tall glass, added some ice, and made our own
blend of juice.

Bernie's favorite drink was a mixture of cranberry juice
and grapefruit juice: *"A virgin sea breeze,"* he said. "That's
what they call it in a bar. Sounds poetic, huh? In the morning, I add fresh-squeezed orange juice to it. Or mango, or
papaya. Sometimes I add ice tea."

It was cool and delicious, the perfect thing to have after
that intense hot tub. We sat in his living room, in front of
the picture window, and gazed at the hills bathed in the
spotlight of a brilliant full moon. It had changed from
orange to silvery white.

We sat quietly, sipping our drinks, watching the silent
moon. There was very little light in the room; the moon
was the star of the show. I felt relaxed, in no hurry to do
anything or go anywhere. I was just content to sit in silence.
That was unusual for me — usually I was rushing along,
always looking ahead, wanting something in the future,
whether it was to finish a project or get to some destination
or get a cup of coffee or the next meal. I so rarely sat still and
just enjoyed being in the present moment, with absolutely
no desire for anything else to make me happy or fulfilled.

Bernie sat motionless. I did too, and seemed to lose
track of time. It seemed as if we sat there for just a few

minutes, though the moon climbed high in the sky. It was getting late.

BERNIE FINALLY MOVED A BIT, took a sip of his juice, and looked at me.

"I want to show you something before you go," he said. His voice was deep and quiet. "You seem to be open to it. I don't show this to many people — it's a course in magic — a course in creation.

"All creation is magical, and we create all the time. So all of us are already magical beings. All of us are magicians. But most of us don't know it, that's all.

"Here's an entire course in magic — it's a short course, but it's all that's necessary. Let's see . . . I need some paper. . . ."

He got up and wandered off into the darkness. He made almost no noise as he moved. When he returned he adjusted the light in the room, turning it up a little. I noticed his lamps had adjustments, so he could control the amount of light each one gave off. He handed me a pen, a sheet of paper, and kept a pen and some paper for himself.

"Draw one of these," he said. And he drew a large star in the center that covered over half the sheet, like this:

"This star is central to this teaching. I use a five-pointed star — you can use a six-pointed star if you wish, or any number of points, or simply a radiant circle. The important thing is to imagine that it's a star, and it's filled with light — shining clearly in front of you.

"Focus on this light-filled star, and let the light take whatever form it will. It may remain as a star, or it may change for you. It may be a person filled with light, with arms outstretched. In Western magic, the five-pointed star stands for Man, with arms outstretched. Man — or Woman — in the form of light, in the form of God, whatever you want to call it.

"This star represents *you*. It's who you are, after all — we're all created from the stuff of stars, as Carl Sagan put it.

"Now, at the top point of this star, put these words:

GOD'S WILL

"Or something similar, however you choose to define God. Choose whatever words work for you, whatever keeps reminding you to turn your desires, your goals, your problems, *everything* over to God as you understand God — the forces of creation.

"At every other point on the star, list something you want to create in your life, something you're passionate about. With a five-pointed star, you choose your top four goals, desires, dreams, and put one at each point.

"Putting it in this visual way works, for many reasons. It forces you, for one thing, to keep asking yourself if what you are wishing for is God's will. It forces you, too, to just choose four possibilities, from the realm of all possibilities. So you have to prioritize: What are your four most important goals?

"Once you have chosen your goals and written them down, affirm to yourself: 'I am now ready and willing to receive what I'm asking for.' Then prepare yourself to receive it, because you're going to receive it.

"Try it and see what happens!

"As Deepak Chopra says, *Within every desire is the seed and mechanics for its fulfillment.*' This is brilliant — the essence of magic.

"It's very similar to what Ralph Waldo Emerson said a long time ago: *You wouldn't have been given your desires in the first place if you didn't have the capability of achieving them.*' Think about these things!

"Fold your paper and carry it with you at all times. Focus on your star often enough to keep it emblazoned in your consciousness. Focus on it until your desires become intentions.

"An intention is much stronger than a desire. We didn't just desire to create the bodies we have today, our DNA is encoded with the absolute intention to create the bodies we have today. Once a desire becomes an intention, about 90 percent of your perceived or imagined obstacles dissolve. And you have the knowledge and strength — the *will* — to deal effectively with the other 10 percent.

"Once your desires become intentions, you will create what you intend to create, no more, and no less. James Allen wrote one of my favorite quotes of all time in *As You Think*: *'You will become as great as your dominant aspiration. . . . If you cherish a vision, a lofty ideal in your heart, you will realize it.'*

"That's Western magic in a nutshell."

I WROTE MY DESIRES at each point of my star. They came quickly, as fast as I could write. Each one led to the next.

When I finished, Bernie asked an unexpected question, something no one had ever asked me, and I had never asked myself:

"How much money do you want to make? How much money is enough?"

"That's a good question, Bernie," I said. "I have to think about that one."

"Here's a good question: Why do you want to make money? What does it represent for you?"

The words just spilled out: "Peace and power," I said. Bernie looked highly amused.

"What do you mean?" he asked.

"A certain level of money would give me a sense of peacefulness; I'd be able to do things at my own pace, in an easy and relaxed manner — the way you seem to work. And it would give me the power to do what I want to do, to fulfill my purpose in life." I had the distinct thought that if we hadn't had such a quiet evening, with so many silences, my words would have been very different — far more superficial.

"Peace and power — that's good!" Bernie said. He had that delighted, almost childlike look again. "All right —

focus on this thought, on this affirmation: *I now have peace and power.* Write it in big letters at the top of your page, above your star. Keep repeating those words: *I now have peace and power.* You don't need a million dollars in the bank before you have peace and power. Keep remembering that affirmation, until your subconscious accepts it and you create it in your life.

"People don't really want money, they want what money can bring to them. Keep affirming you already have peace and power — or whatever it may be — and you'll have it!"

He laughed like a little child, utterly pleased with himself. "Got it?"

"Got it."

I DROVE HOME IN A STRANGE STATE — it was almost euphoria, though maybe that's too strong a word. I felt serene, completely content to be myself, doing exactly what I was doing in that moment.

I drove in silence — no radio or music, which I almost always played as I drove. I was perfectly content to be cruising down the road gazing silently at a world bathed in the silver light of a full moon.

I was at peace.

SUMMARY

- Business, like the rest of life, has a spiritual and mystical side. It used to be that science and religion or metaphysics were considered to be almost polar opposites. But in the twentieth century, science and metaphysics merged. Physicists tell us what the metaphysical types have been saying for centuries: We are in reality all one, in one vast quantum field, eternally interconnected with everything else in the universe.

- There is nothing new in the New Age: The so-called New Age philosophy is the Perennial Philosophy that Aldous Huxley described — it's as old as humankind, and taught in Christianity, Eastern traditions, and other religions and indigenous cultures throughout the world.

- Eastern traditions teach about *dharma* — the laws of the universe, and the importance for each of us to discover our higher purpose in life, our mission, and to fulfill that purpose.

- Eastern traditions as well as Christianity teach about *karma* — all of us are rewarded with the fruits of our thoughts and actions, whether those thoughts and actions are good or bad. As you sow, so shall you reap.

- Indigenous peoples all over the world teach us that the earth is sacred, the earth is our Mother, and we must respect and cherish her.

- The 12-step programs have brilliant wisdom for the modern world, as well. They encourage us to keep turning our life and our will over to the care of God, as we understand God. Everyone has some conception of God, or a higher power, or the creative force of the universe, or the Great Mystery. Whenever you have a problem — business or personal — turn it over to the forces of creation, to God as you understand God. Let God work out the details. You will be shown, step by step, intuitively, what to do. It will involve these two powerful and practical words: *love and serve.* Love and serve yourself and others — this is a great key to the greatest success you can imagine.

- All creation is magical, and we create all the time. So all of us are already magicians — though a lot of us don't know it. Visualizing your goals is a powerful form of magic. Deepak Chopra wrote, "Within every desire is the seed and mechanics for its fulfillment." This is the essence of magic.

- As James Allen wrote, "You will become as great as your dominant aspiration. . . . If you cherish a vision, a lofty ideal in your heart, you will realize it."

- Why do you want to make money? It's not just to have money in the bank; it's for some other, better reason. What do you want money to bring you? Whatever your answer may be, affirm that you have it *now*, and see what happens. Do you want money so you'll have peace and power in your life?

Affirm, repeatedly and with energy: *"I now have peace and power."* And you'll discover a peace and power within you that has nothing to do with the amount of money you have in your bank or investment portfolio.

KEY TWELVE

Do what you love to do,
and you'll create a visionary business,
in your own absolutely unique way.

A LONG AND DIFFICULT WINTER PASSED, and I didn't hear a word from Bernie. We weathered the storms all right, though — I prayed a lot. We even got fairly close to our projections. There was some of Bernie's magic involved.

I made notes from everything I could remember Bernie had said and typed them up so I could keep referring to his words and remembering them. It was far too easy to forget all the things he said and go back to old patterns of behavior, the old ways of thinking that focused on the problems rather than the opportunities, the habitual ways of thinking and acting that involved struggle and frustration and failure. But I used Bernie's magic. I carried the star that I had drawn around with me, and reflected on it now and then. I sat in silence occasionally and meditated on it for a little while. I affirmed *I now have peace and power*. It felt wonderful — *empowering* — every time I said those words to myself.

One goal I had written on the star was the income we had projected for that year. We almost hit it — we were a bit short, but close enough for satisfaction. We had almost doubled the previous year's sales.

SPRING FINALLY CAME, late and sudden, warm and sunny, with flowers blooming in places I had never noticed before. Bernie called one Friday afternoon and asked if I would like to come over. I told him I would love to. I had no idea what to expect.

It was late afternoon by the time I got there, and we sat on his back porch, drank coffee, and looked at the view. His yard was filled with flowers, sloping down over a hill with a view of eternity.

The front door chimed. It turned out to be someone delivering an international feast Bernie had ordered. Lucia joined us, her clothes speckled with dozens of colors of paint, and we had a delicious dinner of many small courses.

"This is a special occasion," Bernie said. "It's been just over a year now that we've known each other. We're celebrating your year of accomplishment. To life, and to your great success."

He toasted me with his sparkling blend of fruit juices. We joined the toast with ours.

"And to you, Bernie, and Lucia," I said, searching for something to say that expressed my feelings. I couldn't think of anything at that moment, though, so I just said, "I wish you good health, happiness, prosperity, and love."

We clinked our glasses together.

"It's good to celebrate your accomplishments," Bernie said. "Take your whole crew out to dinner when you achieve your goals. And give them a nice bonus check.

"You're well on your way now. You've got all the tools you need. Keep learning new things, always, from everyone and everything you can. And keep reinventing your business. It's a never-ending process. It keeps growing, organically, like every other living thing, in its own way, in its perfect own time.

"Learn from those who have been successful in your field. In every field, there have been great successes, and a lot of failures. Focus on the successful people. Get to know them, if you can. Read about them. Study their methods. You'll create your own methods to become successful, but never lose sight of others in the field who have already created their success.

"Celebrate their success. And learn from it."

He took a great sip of his fruit juice, then continued.

"Celebrate the success of your competitors, too. And even celebrate those who might think they're your enemies as well. You don't have to get down on their level; you don't have to compete with others or fight with others. You don't need any enemies, and you don't have to have any enemies — it's up to you. *Love your enemies*, Jesus said. If you do, you don't have any enemies, do you?

"It's an abundant universe; in an abundant universe we

don't have to compete for survival. There's plenty to go around. Competition — in any negative way — and animosity don't have to exist in your world. Celebrate the success of others — it'll help you create even more of your own success.

"You've got all the tools you need now. I've passed on everything I can. You know how to create a vision of a business that is successful, and how to focus on that vision and manifest it, with a great deal of help from your higher power, or God, or the creative power of the universe, or your intuitive mind, or whatever you want to call it."

He paused, and thought for a moment.

"I just have one more thing to say to you:

"Remember what Joseph Campbell said: *'Follow your bliss.'* Do what you love to do! Work with passion, live with passion, and you'll create a visionary business, in your own absolutely unique way.

"I look forward to having dinner with you again in another year — and hearing you tell me you've doubled your sales again, and are solidly profitable."

"That's our goal," I said.

"So be it, so it is," said Bernie, with surprising force.

I LEFT NOT LONG AFTER DINNER. As I headed across the lawn toward my car, Bernie called out from the front door.

"Oh, one more thing. A little present." He disappeared back into the house and returned with a small box wrapped in shiny silver-colored paper.

I opened it right away. It was a piece of polished wood

designed to sit on a desk or table, with these words inscribed
on a brass plate:

Keep away from people who try to belittle your ambitions.
Small people do that, but the really great make you feel that
you, too, can somehow become great.

— MARK TWAIN

I was touched by his gift, and by the sweet, fumbling
way he gave it to me. As I started to thank him, my eyes
suddenly filled with tears.

SUMMARY

- Keep learning new things, always, from everyone and everything you can. And keep reinventing your business. It is a never-ending process. It keeps growing, organically, like every other living thing, in its own way, in its own perfect time.

- We live in an abundant universe; in an abundant universe we don't have to compete with anyone for survival. There is plenty to go around. Competition — in any negative way — and animosity don't have to exist in your world. Celebrate the success of others — it will help you create even more of your own success.

- You don't have to have any enemies in your life — it's up to you. *"Love your enemies,"* Jesus said. If you do, you don't have any enemies, do you?

- Remember what Joseph Campbell said: *"Follow your bliss."* Do what you love to do! Work with passion, live with passion, and you'll create a visionary business, in your own absolutely unique way.

- "Keep away from people who try to belittle your ambitions," Mark Twain once wrote. "Small people do that, but the really great make you feel that you, too, can somehow become great."

EPILOGUE

The ultimate purpose of visionary business
is to transform the world by doing
what you love to do.

THE PAGES THAT FOLLOW were originally in the last chapter (chapter 12) in early drafts of this book. Several early readers of the manuscript, however, had objections to the material.

Some of them felt the material wasn't relevant to the book; they saw the book as primarily for those who want to focus on their own businesses and who aren't yet ready to transform the world. Another reader said, interestingly enough, "If you leave it in there, you'll lose the East Coast." I don't know if either comment is valid, but I ended up making a compromise — it was my friend Kent Nerburn's idea, actually — that allows me to take the material out of the book and leave it in at the same time: I'm including it as an epilogue for you to read or to ignore, as you see fit.

I feel that this material is an important part of this book. It applies all the ideas of this work in another important arena: global transformation.

Over the years since this was first written, I've come to see Bernie's elaborate story as a fantasy, and as a metaphor for what is actually now taking place. At first, I seriously considered starting a nonprofit organization based on his ideas, but then I realized it wasn't necessary: it is already happening globally in the work of over a million nonprofit organizations. As Buckminster Fuller pointed out, *the infrastructure is already in place.* The work simply needs to be supported by far more people — and every one of us can do something to contribute in some way to making our world a better place for those who follow in our footsteps.

WE SAT ON BERNIE'S BACK PORCH, drank a blend of fruit juices, and looked at the view of the nearby flowers, the distant hills, and the eternal skies with their ever-shifting clouds.

Bernie didn't say a word for a while. We looked at the view and felt the wind in our faces. Then he said, "Sometimes I fantasize about writing a novel. But it's so much work to write a novel! So I ask myself, why bother?"

(That was one of the very few negative things I ever heard Bernie say. It wasn't until many years later that I discovered he had written several books.)

"But I've got the story in my mind," he continued, "and I keep adding to it, filling it out. It's a Utopian novel — there hasn't been a good Utopian novel written in years.

"It's based on this fact: With enough money and creativity, every major problem in the world can be solved.

"As Buckminster Fuller said, '*We have the technology to solve the world's problems.*' We just haven't used our technology skillfully enough.

"One of the world's major problems is that it's still trapped in *poverty consciousness*: Most people — and almost all nations, it seems — feel there really isn't enough money to go around. But, contrary to most people's beliefs, there is plenty of money: Money is readily available, if we know how to manifest it. There's *plenty* of money available, it's just not being distributed very well.

"Money is just like food — in fact, the two are interchangeable. There is plenty of food in the world, but it's not being distributed to the people who need it. There's plenty of money in the world, but not enough of it is getting to the people who need it.

"We don't lack for money — all we lack is understanding and creativity. All we lack is *vision*.

"One person's vision can change the world — that's been proven in the past. And that's what my novel is about. Do you want to hear about it?"

"Sure!"

"It starts with a young man or a young woman, it doesn't matter which. I'm not sure yet which it'll be, but it'll be some young person who creates a vital part of a new technology, builds a big business around it, and in a decade or so is worth billions.

"He — or she — gets married to a mystical person from South America, or Africa, and together they form the most creative financial team the world has ever seen. Every year their assets double — in spite of the fact that they spend massive amounts of money every year, supporting other people in becoming successful.

"The woman gets pregnant, and strange omens begin to happen. Flowers bloom out of season. Music is heard in the wind, by people all over the community. An owl comes to guard their door. The woman has identical twins, a boy and a girl. There are miracle stories about their early years; they exhibit human and psychic powers far more quickly than other children.

"Many more brothers and sisters are born, until there are a total of twelve — six boys and six girls — and as soon as they're old enough to leave home, they spread over the earth, carrying the vision of their parents: a vision of a world that works.

"The children go light-years beyond their parents in financial success and power to create change for the better. All the children are complete, natural masters of both fund-raising and diplomacy. They create a vast worldwide non-profit organization, dedicated to improving the quality of life for all, that affects every person on earth.

"The organization is called FOCI — that's the plural of focus (pronounced FO-sigh) — the Foundation of Creative

Individuals. Its purpose is to awaken the creativity inherent in all of us, and help us all creatively solve our problems, whatever they may be — whether they're basic problems of food and shelter or more complex problems of education, recovery and therapy, or fulfilling artistic or business dreams.

"The Foundation becomes the most powerful nonprofit organization the world has ever imagined, more powerful than most governments. Hundreds of millions of people contribute to it, because it helps so many people in so many ways.

"All over the world — eventually in some form in every populated area — a great school system is built, with well-paid — *highly* paid — teachers and with great resources for the students. Everyone has access to an excellent education — and it's free, from day care and preschool to graduate school. Centers of arts, sports, and learning are established all over the world.

"Simultaneously, there are massive efforts to place a safety net under the global population: to house and feed the homeless and heal the sick and addicted and support others who need it.

"The common goal of the Foundation of Creative Individuals is to stimulate everyone's creativity: Every person in the community is invited to develop and express their own unique creativity, and they're assisted in all kinds of ways in doing just that.

"The goal is to encourage everyone to creatively solve their problems, and then to unleash their creativity in other arenas: artistic and business and humanitarian.

"The mother, father, and twins become known as the Quartet, the visionary leaders of the Foundation. The mother and father maintain and build their private wealth, and fund the nonprofit corporation that way, while the children work within the Foundation.

"Each of the twelve children is given a territory, and they leave no part of the earth uncovered. In a few short years, their impact is global.

"The group empowers the individual. It is set up like Alcoholics Anonymous — no one governs anyone. The leaders are but trusted servants; they do not govern. Everyone is invited to participate in their own unique way.

"FOCI, of course, focuses on many different things: every level of human endeavor, every level of Abraham Maslow's pyramid. Are you familiar with Maslow's pyramid of human consciousness? Those on the bottom need food and shelter. If you don't have food and shelter, your efforts to get them are all-consuming. Those a step above are concerned with security. Those above them are free to work on their education and their personal problems, their recovery and health issues. Those near the top are free to focus on their creative expression, and their fulfillment in life.

"FOCI operates on all these levels. Those on the first levels, needing food, shelter, and security, are supported. Those who want or need recovery and other types of therapy can go to a wide range of counselors and free programs and support groups — *everyone* is encouraged to go to some kind of program, if they wish. There's free health care for all

— something every government can afford to provide its people. And the vast numbers who need to improve their education are supported in doing so by a well-funded educational system.

"Those with creative dreams, dreams of personal fulfillment, are supported by the arts and sports centers and universities and business schools. The current institutions of learning are strengthened, and many more new ones spring up everywhere.

"There's even a Bernie's School of Business — it's named after me for dreaming all this up. It's a franchise operation, with branches all over the world, where they study my business methods and finance thousands — *millions* — of people who go into business for themselves.

"The art schools and business schools support and finance the dreams of those who wish to attend. Here's where a tremendous amount of energy and money is generated. Artists and businesspeople are shown how to be successful — however they want to define success. Artists are taught how to create business plans and finance their projects — millions of limited partnerships are created! One of the major purposes of FOCI is teaching people to write business plans, and then financing those plans, often picking up 25 to 50 percent equity in the projects. A lot of those projects make substantial money, and once the artists and businesspeople are successful, they give generously back to the organization.

"FOCI supports every genuine environmental and human rights organization. All current structures working for good are strengthened: nonprofit organizations, schools, sports centers, art centers, health-care centers, youth centers, child-care centers, and so on.

"At first it works independently from any official government, but eventually it works in partnership with every government on earth, because the people involved in the Foundation have enough money and power to creatively buy their way out of all of the problems of the world. The goal, the dream, is Utopian, after all: to create a world that works for every one of its people, a world of opportunity and creative expression. Who wouldn't want that?

"FOCI united with governments build campuses all over the world that are centers of learning and diplomatic centers as well, where they negotiate with local people and world leaders alike. Over a period of only twenty years, they creatively solve a great many of the world's major problems — homelessness, starvation, war, drug abuse, violence, environmental destruction, extinction of wildlife and plants. It's all accomplished through the use of the vast sums of private wealth from the family and millions of other contributors as well as the profits the businesses generate.

"Part of their magic is that nearly everywhere FOCI invests, they eventually make profits. Those who are educated for free, for example, donate generously after they start making money. Artists and businesspeople who receive backing and guidance from the organization give back to it once they are successful. Those who have been helped by FOCI, or just wish to support the goals of FOCI, are encouraged to donate at least 5 percent of their income to FOCI, and another 5 percent to other good causes.

"FOCI invests roughly a third of their resources into helping those at the bottom of the pyramid get food, shelter, and security; a third into helping those in the middle who want education, health care, and therapy; and a third into assisting those at the top realize their dreams of business or artistic success or humanitarian work.

"They feed the hungry, with a global network of food distribution so that there is plenty of food for all who need it. In the process, farmers are supported as well, for FOCI buys the food at prices the farmers can live well on.

"They build shelters for the poor. They convert old military bases and old navy ships into housing, hospitals, and schools for those who need them and want them.

"They invest in the inner cities, rebuilding youth centers that grow into centers of creative expression, and rebuilding schools that evolve into centers of free higher education, training children during the day and adults at night and on weekends to discover their creativity and talents and ways to support themselves abundantly. What a concept! It's called a public education system.

"They buy back the rainforests and vast tracts of other land and give them back to the indigenous people. They reeducate loggers and hunters and others who are creating environmental problems, and support them until they can move into new jobs and careers that are not destructive to animals or to the environment. They help businesses that are environmentally destructive — including oil companies — to develop new products and services that don't harm the environment.

"They develop solar energy, solar vehicles, clean fuels. . . .

"They face a vast number of challenges and difficulties, of course, requiring the reeducation of literally billions of people. But the single vision of the leaders is contagious, and it spreads around the world.

"The movement is aided by a new generation of children, who are born with an innate sensitivity for the health of the planet. They become powerful environmentalists; the force of the children crying for change makes changes — gradually, organically — in the way things operate. I think this is now happening, and the younger generation will make environmentally aware career choices and will have a powerful impact on all of our destructive business practices.

"The generation that follows that one says to their elders, 'Thanks for cleaning up the planet, but you haven't done enough for human-rights abuses — and abuses to all other living creatures.' And that generation creates a world in which every human being — as well as every animal, plant, and rock — is respected and cherished for its own unique creative nature, its own sacred way of being.

"They become the leaders of a new renaissance, where individual creativity flourishes, environmental balance is restored, and the world is united in peace. A revolution takes place, through natural growth and evolution, without violence. The result is something all of us want, certainly: *peace and prosperity.*

"I'm convinced that, with enough money and vision, it can be done. And there is plenty of money out there — there is an abundance of money in this world. So the only thing missing is the vision. . . .

"Remember the words of Charles Colton: *'If universal charity prevailed, Earth would be a heaven, and Hell a fable.'*"

BERNIE STARED into the shape-shifting clouds, intensely, wistfully. The spring sun illuminated his face. He looked the part of the visionary.

"All you need is the vision," he repeated. "Then anything is possible. The details will all get worked out, one way or another, once we make a clear goal of creating a world that works for everyone.

"The book has a message: The ultimate purpose of visionary business is not to make money; it is to transform the world, by doing what we love to do and what we need to do to bring about a new era of peace and prosperity for all."

Bernie had once again given me plenty of food for thought.

SUMMARY

- One of the world's major problems is that it is trapped in "poverty consciousness" — most people, and almost all nations, feel there really isn't enough money to go around. But contrary to most people's beliefs, there is plenty of money: Money is readily available; we simply have a distribution problem. Not enough money or food is getting to the people who need it.

- With enough money and creativity, every major problem the world now faces can be solved. One person's vision can change the world — that has been proven in the past.

- The ultimate purpose of visionary business is not to make money; it is to transform the world by doing what we love to do and what we need to do to bring about a new era of peace and prosperity for all.

AFTERWORD TO THE REVISED EDITION

Develop the three essentials of success,
in an easy and relaxed manner,
a healthy and positive way.

I T IS NOW WELL OVER TWENTY-FIVE YEARS since I met Bernie. He passed away years ago. Sometimes I imagine — sometimes I am quite sure — that he's well aware of this book and he's getting a great many chuckles out of it all.

My company has grown and prospered. It is a good example of teamwork and partnership. It shows that the keys Bernie gave me are effective, and that *anyone* — even someone as clueless as I was — can build a successful company.

I dreamed of my ideal scene, and that dream came to be. It took me about ten years to realize the ideal life I imagined I could have in five years. Many things took longer to develop than I hoped, but we eventually got to where we wanted to be.

I made a list of my goals, and read each one at least a few times a week, and affirmed it was coming to be *in an easy and relaxed manner, in a healthy and positive way.* Sometimes I would add *in its own perfect time, for the highest good of all.* At the end I added, *This, or something better, is now manifesting, in totally satisfying and harmonious ways, for the highest good of all.*

Every goal on that list came true, in an easy and relaxed manner, in a healthy and positive way. Over the years, I realized that simply repeating those words to myself a few thousand times overcame a huge number of my doubts and fears, because those doubts and fears certainly whispered, *It won't be easy, it's difficult; it won't be relaxed, it's all so stressful! Maybe it's not even healthy, or positive.*

Affirming that phrase over and over confronted and contradicted and eventually changed a great many of my deepest and least helpful beliefs. I told myself, over and over, *I am creating the life of my dreams, in an easy and relaxed manner, in a healthy and positive way.* This is a powerful affirmation.

OVER THE YEARS, it's all definitely gotten easier and easier. The pace of my life has slowed way down. I have lots of time for myself, and for family and friends. Several days each week I have absolutely nothing on my schedule. I have proven to myself that it is possible to start and build a successful company without being a Type A or a workaholic. It is possible to succeed and still have a life outside the business — a creative life, a family life, and a spiritual life as well. *A life of leisure* — that's a dream come true for me.

We all know that work expands to fill the time we give it — yet most of us still work far too hard. I've proven you can build a successful company in a relaxed manner, with a lot of vacations throughout the year and, even better, mini-vacations each week.

Most people seem shocked when I tell them my schedule — a lot of them don't think it's possible, apparently, and have never even considered something like it. I don't do mornings, or Mondays. And I never work on Sunday. I'm at the office usually at 1:00 or 2:00 in the afternoon on Tuesday through Thursday or Friday.

With the schedule I have, every day of the week has become my favorite day, but if I had to pick one day, I'd pick Monday. I start the week by taking Mondays off. I never have any plans on Monday, except to relax and meditate at some point (almost always flat on my back), and to have dinner with my family and be with my wife and son in the evening.

Throughout the week, I take all the mornings off as well. I have never been a morning person. I almost never schedule anything before noon, and usually sleep until 10:00 or 11:00 AM.

I work between fifteen and twenty-five hours a week, typically, at my company. I can live with that schedule. Someone once told me I was semiretired — and I said, "I'll never retire! I'm doing what I love to do, so why would I ever quit doing it?" I've just set it up so I work when I feel like it and do other things (or nothing at all) when I don't feel like working. That just seems sensible to me.

I put my son to bed almost every night. I spend about

thirty hours a week with my family on average — more time than I spend at the office and as much time as I spend alone.

This is the kind of balance that works for me. I encourage everyone to think creatively about their schedule, and make the adjustments necessary to have a *life* as well as a career, a life that includes time for yourself and your creative expression and your family and friends.

THE THREE ESSENTIALS
OF SUCCESS

OVER THE YEARS I HAVE HAD A LOT OF FEEDBACK on this book. Most of it has been very good; many of the stories about what people have done after reading this book are what I call miracle stories.

One woman woke her husband up at 3:00 in the morning after she finished *Visionary Business* and told him, "I'm going to double our sales in three months." She was working on her dream, her own retail shop, selling the things she loved, but it had been a struggle every step of the way. She knew if she doubled her sales, she would be cruising along profitably and would be able to do substantial profit sharing with all her employees. Within three months, she had doubled her sales.

I've heard story after story like that. Those stories make it all worthwhile for me.

Some people have wanted more from this book, however. One reviewer wrote that he wanted more specific information about what I went through as I built my company. I've given that a lot of thought, and here's what I've come to feel:

The specifics of my particular company are completely different from yours. Each industry, each trade has its own rules of operation and its own skills to master. Each individual business has its own unique challenges that require creativity and flexibility.

The answers to all those specific questions you have are right in front of you, at every moment. Exactly how do you set up your business? Go ask someone in your community who has done it. Or just get on the Internet. The specific details are things you discover as you go along. It's obvious how to find out the information you need to know once you start asking for it. People love to share this kind of information.

The important things to remember, always, are your dream and your plan. Keep your inner eye on the big picture, and sooner or later, one way or another, you'll get there.

There are just three things you need to fulfill your dream and become successful in business or as an artist. None of these three things are all that difficult to attain. They don't require any higher math or college degree. Every business, every person with a successful career, and every successful artist has these three simple things together to some degree:

1. Your Product or Service

This one is obvious, right? And yet a lot of people spend their lives focused on creating a product or service that doesn't serve them very well and doesn't serve others very well either, or else is so much less than it could have been. Most people simply do not think expansively enough when it comes to creating a product or service.

The key to real success and fulfillment here is to *do what you love to do*. Find out what you are passionate about, and find how to become successful doing what you love to do. Think in expansive terms.

Whatever you can dream of doing, being, and having, there are many, many others who have done it successfully, and been it, and have it or had it. Look at those who have succeeded doing what you love. If they can do it, it shows you it can be done. If you're persistent, focused on your goal, you can find a way to get there, sooner or later.

Do what you love to do,
and keep doing it, with persistence.
And don't dream too small.

2. Marketing and Sales

This one is obvious as well: Whatever product or service you have, you need to find a way to present it to the world and be well paid for it.

The key to success here is to *have a multipronged strategy that doesn't take no for an answer*. What do I mean by multipronged? It means that you realize there are countless different ways you can market and sell your work. Try the most obvious one; if that doesn't work, try another. If that doesn't work, try something else.

Look at people who have been successful and try what has worked for them. If that doesn't work, try something totally new, something completely out of the box. Don't forget the Internet: through the Internet, you have the whole world at your fingertips.

As Bert Lahr, the comedian in *The Wizard of Oz*, said, "Stay on the merry-go-round long enough, and you're bound to catch the brass ring, sooner or later." Be persistent. Don't give up.

Another key: Be sure to price your work high enough so that it works for you. Several years ago, we got permission from an artist to use one of her paintings on a book cover. I got to know her, and she was struggling to pay the rent every month in her little studio apartment. She was selling her originals for a only few hundred dollars, and I said she should raise her prices.

She said, "How much? A thousand dollars?" That was a scary stretch for her. I said, "Your paintings are beautiful. Charge five thousand, or ten thousand."

She went away in a state of shock. But she called me a few weeks later, overjoyed, saying, "You won't believe this — I just sold a painting for *ten thousand dollars!*" I did believe it; I know plenty of people, including myself, who would rather pay ten thousand for an original work of art than just a few hundred.

I once heard a great piece of advice: If someone doesn't complain that you are charging too much for your work, then you aren't charging enough for your work. Value your time and energy, and you will receive value for it.

Develop a multipronged strategy
to sell and market your work.
Value your work, and be persistent.

3. Financial Controls

As it is for many artists and entrepreneurs, this was the last piece of the puzzle I was able to put into place. I had good products very early on, and after a few years and several expensive mistakes, I finally found the right sales and marketing team to get my work out into the marketplace and sell it effectively.

But we still lost money, month after month, for our first five years. Why? I had never even heard the expression "financial controls." We were operating by the seat of our pants, as the phrase goes, and our expenses kept exceeding our income.

Finally, the right person came along and showed me what good financial controls were. It simply means this (and it was a new concept to me at the time): Watch your expenses carefully; move as quickly as you can to get to a place where your expenses are less than your income.

This is not rocket science; this is not a difficult concept. Yet so many businesses, large and small, have blown it because they haven't had financial controls.

After five years of losses, we hired a new bookkeeper. She turned out to be far more than just a bookkeeper: She became a key executive, because her contribution was a key to our success. She had never worked for a publisher before, so she researched our industry by reading various trade magazines. Then one day, she walked into our office with a single sheet of paper.

"Here's what your problem is, Marc," she said. The paper had two columns: On the left was our income at the top for the past year, and below was listed all our expenses, broken up into four main categories: Editorial, Production, Marketing, and G&A (General and Administrative, usually called "overhead"). Not only had she listed the actual expenses below each head, but she had also calculated the percentage of income we were spending in each category: Editorial, 45%; Production, 38%; Marketing, 2%; G&A, 25%.

Under the main categories, the expenses were further broken up into very specific categories: Salaries, freelance editors and artists, rent, office supplies, postage, and so forth. Each was listed as a dollar amount and also as a percentage of the total income for the year.

In the column on the right, she had industry averages for all those expenses for a company our size. So she compared every one of our expenses with the industry average: Editorial, 25%; Production, 30%; Marketing, 10%; G&A, 25%.

It was right there in undeniable black and white: "Here's what your problem is, Marc — you're spending way too much on Editorial and too much on Production. We're not spending enough on Marketing, and our G&A is just about right in line."

Even someone as clueless as I was at the time could do the math — and she had totaled it up at the bottom to make it even easier: Our expenses in the four categories equaled 110 percent of our sales, meaning we were spending $1.10 for every dollar of sales. Industry averages for the four categories totaled 90 percent of sales, meaning they were making ten cents for every dollar of sales.

All we needed to do was get our costs in alignment with industry averages, and we would be profitable. It wasn't all that difficult to do once we could see where we needed to make those adjustments: We simply couldn't spend so much money editing or printing our books.

We made some necessary changes, and within a few months, we were profitable. We've been operating ever since with solid financial controls.

I finally realized this: *With good financial controls, you can succeed at a very modest level of income.* It all depends on your expenses. The more you can keep your expenses down, the sooner you'll be profitable and the fatter those profits will be.

> *Institute good financial controls:*
> *Monitor every expense*
> *and make sure those expenses*
> *remain well below your income.*

That's all that is necessary: a product or service you love, a way to market it successfully, and financial controls. None of these three things is particularly difficult. Each of them, though, does require a different type of focus and energy at different times.

I personally have very little interest in marketing and sales or financial number crunching. Once my company started growing, I found the right people who saw the great opportunities for them in helping me fulfill those functions. If you're an artist or a small, one-person operation, you may have to sit down with yourself occasionally and "put on your marketing hat" and become your own marketing director. And periodically — maybe a day every six months would even be enough — you've got to sit down and become your own Chief Financial Officer and add up all your income and expenses for the previous year, and project your income and expenses for the next year, and make sure your expenses are in line.

Or perhaps you can work with a good bookkeeper who can do the number crunching for you and help you with the analysis. This is some of the most important work you can do.

DARE TO DREAM

THE MOST IMPORTANT WORK, of course, is this: *Dare to dream*. Dream your most expansive dream, dream of the ideal life you want to create for yourself in five or ten years. Write that dream down. There is great power in the written word.

Make a plan on how you can reach that dream, and write it down too, on just a page or two of paper. Then take the first obvious step you need to take, then the next, then the next.

Be persistent, and never lose sight of your dream, your goals, and your plan to reach those goals.

Dare to dream — and go for it!
You'll never regret it.

SUMMARY

*Twenty-five Principles and Practices
of Visionary Business*

1. Every company needs a solid, well-written business plan that charts a clear course for the next year, first in words, then in numbers. A well-written plan is your map, your visualization of the future.

2. The business plan should start with a one-page summary, and then include a brief, concise mission statement that is idealistic and grand.

3. Before writing the business plan, do the "ideal scene" process: Assume five years have passed, and your business has succeeded brilliantly, as well as you can possibly imagine: What would you like to be doing? What is your ideal scene? If you could have exactly the kind of life you wanted, what would it

be? Put it in writing, and compare it with others involved in your business.

4. Plan on everything in a start-up business to take twice as long and cost twice as much as you expect. Make sure you have — or are asking for — plenty of capital, enough to cover every imaginable contingency. Add another 15 percent on top of all projected expenses for contingencies.

5. Your plan has to be strong enough to overcome every possible hurdle and obstacle, external and internal: external problems such as lack of capital, changes in the marketplace and economy, and competition, as well as your own internal obstacles of fear, doubt, lack of self-esteem, or lack of experience and knowledge. A business plan is powerful, because it sets in motion your powerful subconscious mind. It brings the fantasy of your "ideal scene" down into concrete terms. Once you have completed it, a vital part of your work is done: Your vision of the future has been clearly drawn. Without a vision of the future, there is no future.

6. Every successful business is based on a vision. Someone has first clearly imagined the growth and development of that business, long before that growth occurred in physical reality. Keep focused on a vision of your success, and you will end up aligning the exact forces you need to bring about your success.

7. You have to have a higher purpose than making

money in a business. When you have a higher purpose, you marshal all kinds of forces behind you that support you in your goal. Money is essential in business, but it is secondary. Each of us has a unique purpose for living, and unique talents and abilities to achieve that purpose. We should spend however much time is necessary to discover our purpose, and to live it. Then, and only then, are we fulfilled in life.

8. For every adversity there is an equal or greater benefit. That is a key to visionary business. Life is always filled with problems, but it is filled with opportunities as well. There are opportunities, always, within every problem. Even in the knocks of life, we can find great gifts.

9. A good manager can take any kind of business and turn it around and make it successful. A poor manager can take any kind of business and run it into the ground. Don't dwell on pictures of failure. Keep picturing success. Spend some time in solitude, every day if you can, reviewing your goals, keeping your dreams fresh in your mind. Plan your work and work your plan.

10. Your success will probably take a different route than you planned. Make a clear plan, a clear path to success, but then be flexible enough to change your plans continually as new problems and obstacles and opportunities and successes arise. Your

business might look totally different in five years than you imagine it will look.

11. Put the company's interests before your own interests, and before the interests of any owners, any employees, or anyone else. Take care of the company, first and foremost, and it will take care of you, and take care of all of its owners and employees and many others as well.

12. Create an employee handbook. Include generous employee benefits: vacations, wellness days, health and dental insurance, a pension plan, and profit sharing. A substantial bonus based on profits gets everyone thinking like an owner. Give away a substantial share of your profits to your employees, and the company will do so well that, in the long run, the owners will make more than if they had kept all the profits. This is win-win profit sharing. Be sure to include every employee in the profit sharing.

13. Only you can create your success, and only you can block your success. If your visualization of success is stronger than your doubts and fears, you will succeed. When your desire becomes an intention, over 90 percent of your perceived obstacles dissolve — and you have the inner resources to effectively handle the obstacles that remain.

14. There are two styles of management: management by crisis and management by goals. Those caught in the management-by-crisis trap get so focused on the day-to-day problems they never have time to step

back and see the big picture. Take time to support
your dreams with concrete, achievable plans. Then
the magic happens: All kinds of forces come into
play and help you manifest your dreams.

15. With ownership comes responsibility. The owners
of a business have a responsibility toward the welfare
of their employees, the community, and the environment. If you can't run a business without exploiting people or polluting the planet, you should not
be in that business in the first place.

16. Give a generous portion of your profits to your people and to organizations working to improve the
world. If every profitable business in the world gave
even just 5 percent of their profits to nonprofit corporations working to help people and the environment, we could end starvation around the world,
house the homeless, and clean up the whole planet.

17. Money is not the final measure of a person's worth
— there are far more important things: the kind
of life we lead; the way we treat others and treat
our environment; the service we do for others; the
amount of love and compassion we have for others;
our purpose in life and the degree to which we fulfill it; our positive contribution to others and to our
planet. These things are what is truly important in
life. These things are the only significant measures of
a person's success.

18. It makes great business sense to follow the three rules
of Pepsico's CEO: (1) love change — we either learn

to love it or resist the inevitable; (2) learn to dance —
our working relationships should be a dance, not a
struggle; (3) leave J. Edgar Hoover behind — hire
good people, clearly define their responsibility, and
let them do it their own way.

19. Hire people who are passionate about their work.
Learn the difference between technicians, managers,
and entrepreneurs, and hire appropriate people to
do what they love to do. Treat them like adults, and
they will act like adults; give them responsibility,
and they will be responsible.

20. Every business reflects the consciousness of the
owner. It is extremely important to reflect on the
people and the events that have shaped our lives,
and discover the core beliefs that we have created for
ourselves because of those people and events. Once
our negative beliefs are identified, they can be let go
of, because they are not true — they are simply self-
fulfilling; they become true if we believe them. It is
far better to nurture the positive beliefs that support
the creative genius within each of us. You are capable of anything; there are no limits to what you can
accomplish — if you believe it to be true.

21. The more you give, the more you receive — and not
just financially. You receive far more important
things as well: satisfaction, fulfillment, joy, and love.

22. The words of Christ are still brilliant today and
should be remembered: *Ask and you shall receive,
seek and you shall find, knock and the door will be
opened unto you.... Judge not, lest you be judged*

.... Love one another.... Love your enemies.... Turn the other cheek.... The Kingdom of Heaven is within.

23. It's invaluable to have some kind of understanding of a higher power in order to gain a broader, more intelligent perspective on life, to help turn problems into opportunities, to help you have a life well lived. Alcoholics Anonymous sums it up simply and clearly for millions of people, and could be helpful for millions more: *I made a decision to turn my will and my life over to the care of God, as I understand God.... I seek through prayer and meditation to improve my conscious contact with God, as I understand God, praying only for knowledge of God's will and the power to carry it out.* A powerful way to be able to create the kind of life experience we dream of is to reflect upon what we believe God to be, and turn to it for guidance and inspiration. Turn everything over to God, and let God work out the details. Keep asking what God's will is, and you will be guided in your business and your life to do exactly the right thing for you.

24. Keep learning about the business from everyone and everything you can. Keep reinventing your company: It is a never-ending process. Celebrate your own success, and the success of others as well. Competition in any negative way and animosity don't even have to exist in your world. Follow your bliss: Do what you love to do, work with passion, live with passion, and you will create a visionary business, in your own absolutely unique way.

25. With enough money and understanding and creativity, every major problem the world now faces can be solved. And money is readily available, when we know how to manifest it. So all we lack is understanding and creativity: All we lack is vision. One person's vision can change the world — that has been proven in the past. Far more than one of us — a vast number of us, millions of us — are now inspiring a New Renaissance around the world. The ultimate purpose of visionary business is not to make money: it is to transform the world, by doing what we love to do and what we need to do to bring about a new era of peace and prosperity for all.

ACKNOWLEDGMENTS

I WOULD LIKE TO THANK Julie Bennett, that publishing wizard (she copublished *50 Simple Things You Can Do to Save the Earth*, among other things), for reading the first draft and telling me to refocus and totally rewrite. Thanks for your honesty and insight.

I'd like to thank Kent Nerburn for reading the second draft and giving me encouragement and insightful feedback as well. We've had over forty pretty remarkable years of friendship and mutual support. I am in awe of his writing ability. *Letters to My Son, Small Graces,* and *Neither Wolf nor Dog* are some of the most beautiful and profound pieces of writing I've ever published. If brilliant, soulful writing determines sales, the books will sell millions of copies over time.

Thanks to Gina Misiroglu for her excellent editing of the final draft. You are one of the finest editors I have ever worked with — sensitive, intuitive, intelligent. Thanks to Paula Dragosh and Kristen Cashman for their perceptive feedback on the revised edition.

Thanks to the whole team at Publishers Group West — our marketing and distribution arm — for your enthusiasm about this book. It was the people at PGW — particularly Charlie Winton, Randy Fleming, Gary Toderoff, Susan Reich, and Mark Ouimet — who felt so strongly about the book they insisted I tour nationally to support it (including Minnesota in a January blizzard — thanks a lot). I appreciate your dedication and, even more, your mastery of the thankless task of distributing books throughout the world. Publishers Group West is a visionary business. I wonder if Charlie Winton knew, when he started selling books out of the trunk of his car, he would one day have a company doing way over a hundred million a year in sales. Somewhere along the line, he learned how to visualize very effectively.

Thanks to Auri, my lovely Brazilian wife, for her love and support, her caffe lattes and fruit juice smoothies, and her passion for Brazilian dance. She's now heading the Brazil Hope Foundation and doing her part to make the world a bit better.

Thanks to Janet Mills for her insightful editorial ideas, and to Becky Benenate for her assistance and support far beyond the call of duty.

And thanks to Bernie Nemerov for believing in a naive

kid, being an entertaining mentor and storyteller, and investing $80,000 in a start-up company led by someone who had absolutely no collateral and hadn't the faintest idea what a balance sheet was or what the phrase *financial controls* meant. This book is a tribute to you, Bernie — somehow I have the feeling you're getting a big laugh out of it, on whatever plane of existence you happen to be at the moment.

And thanks finally to a power far beyond me who is really guiding the whole show. It's a great relief to know I'm not in charge, and all I need to do is to keep turning my problems — I mean, my challenges and opportunities — over to a higher power and listening for guidance. You've never failed me yet, and I know you never will.

Thanks to all...

SUGGESTED READING

The Architecture of All Abundance: Seven Foundations to Prosperity, by Lenedra J. Carroll. The mother and manager of the singer Jewel has written one of the most powerful guides to a well-lived life I have ever read. This should be a classic and should be taught in high schools and universities.

The Art of True Healing: The Unlimited Power of Prayer and Visualization, by Israel Regardie. A short book that is the finest course in Western magic that I've ever found. Contains a simple practice you can do lying on your back that can heal your body and attract to you whatever you want in life.

As You Think, by James Allen. Written in 1904 — originally titled *As a Man Thinketh* — it is the granddaddy of inspirational and transformational literature. Brief, concise, and brilliant, this book will show you that "you will become as great as your dominant aspiration. If you cherish a vision, a lofty ideal in your heart, you will realize it."

Creating Affluence, by Deepak Chopra. A modern magician blends Eastern philosophy with Western science and shows us "within every desire is the seed and mechanics for its fulfillment."

Creative Visualization, by Shakti Gawain. A classic, and for good reason: It shows us how, easily and effortlessly, to create what we want in life. This book should be taught in every school in the world, in the seventh or eighth grade.

Five Wishes: How Answering One Simple Question Can Make Your Dreams Come True, by Gay Hendricks. A simple and brilliant little book that can show you the way to realizing the life of your dreams.

The Greatest Secret of All: Moving Beyond Abundance to a Life of True Fulfillment, by Marc Allen. Part 1 of this powerful little book is a concise summary of the "secret" of financial success; part 2 goes way beyond that and gives us the far more important secrets of a life well lived, filled with happiness, inner peace, and ease.

Letters to My Son, by Kent Nerburn. If you are a parent, here's a beautiful collection of all the advice you would want to give to your child. Heartfelt, meaningful. The work of a great soul.

The Message of a Master: A Classic Tale of Wealth, Wisdom, and the Secret of Success, by John McDonald. A powerful work for the aspiring businessperson — or anyone who aspires. Written in 1934, and still visionary today.

The Millionaire Course: A Visionary Plan for Creating the Life of Your Dreams, by Marc Allen. This contains everything I have ever learned that took me from poverty to prosperity and fulfillment. This book should be taught in our high schools — so that every student would leave school with a solid, written plan and the intention as well as the tools to create the most fulfilling life imaginable.

Money Magic: Unleashing Your True Potential for Prosperity and Fulfillment, by Deborah L. Price. If you have difficulty attracting or managing money, this book can be a tremendous help. It can show you how to become a "money magician."

The Power of Now: A Guide to Spiritual Enlightenment, by Eckhart Tolle. This is simply the clearest, most brilliant book I have ever read. It has lightened my life immeasurably and helped millions of others live a far more balanced and joyful life. If you're a Christian, you'll find that Eckhart's explanations of Christ's teachings give them a new depth and power. If you have studied Buddhism, you'll find the book to be a profound translation of Buddha's teachings into language we can all understand and apply in our lives.

The Power of Partnership: Seven Relationships That Will Change Your Life, by Riane Eisler. Creating success in every area of life means creating successful partnerships in every area. Riane Eisler shows us exactly how to do that in all our relationships: with ourselves, our family and friends, our work and community, our nation, our world, nature, and spirit. Filled with brilliant insight; essential reading for the twenty-first century.

The Seven Spiritual Laws of Success, by Deepak Chopra. If you aren't effortlessly, joyously succeeding in life, it is simply because you have forgotten one (or more) of the laws of success. A brilliant work that sums it all up.

Stillness Speaks, by Eckhart Tolle. Just reading the first page of this book (or of *The Power of Now*) will show you why Eckhart Tolle is perhaps the finest teacher now on earth of the transcendent truths of our lives.

The Ten Percent Solution: Seven Steps to Improve Our Lives and Our World, by Marc Allen. This short, powerful book gives us a plan that not only helps us achieve financial security but also makes the world a better place. It shows us how, in very simple language, to become part of the solution to the world's problems, rather than part of the problem.

The Type-Z Guide to Success: A Lazy Person's Manifesto for Wealth and Fulfillment, by Marc Allen. Whether you're a workaholic Type A or a lazy Type Z, this little book can show you how to build a successful career without compromising your values or ignoring what is really important in life, such as your family, creativity, and spirit.

A Visionary Life: Conversations on Personal and Planetary Evolution, by Marc Allen. This continues the story of *Visionary Business* and shows you how to clarify what you want in life and how to create it. It is both inspirational and practical.

Work with Passion: How to Do What You Love for a Living, by Nancy Anderson. A master career consultant shows us how to do what we love for a living. This book is for all those who have trouble discovering their passion and purpose in life.

ABOUT THE AUTHOR

M̲ARC ALLEN IS COFOUNDER (with Shakti Gawain) and president of New World Library. He is the author of several books, including *The Millionaire Course: A Visionary Plan for Creating the Life of Your Dreams* and *The Greatest Secret of All: Moving Beyond Abundance to a Life of True Fulfillment*. He is also a musician and composer, and has recorded several albums of music, including *Solo Flight*, *Petals*, *Breathe*, and his latest, *Awakening*. He lives with his wife and son in Marin County, California, where he conducts live seminars and teleconferences, including a free teleconference every month.

For details, see his website: www.MarcAllen.com.